The
HIDDEN PLACES
of
SOMERSET

including Exmoor and the Mendips

Edited by
Shane Scott

CONTENTS

CHAPTER ONE
Bath & Northeast Somerset

Royal Crescent, Bath

1
Bath & Northeast Somerset

Bath

Bath is one of the most remarkable cities in Britain. It is a glorious concoction of architectural set-pieces which have been constructed around the only hot thermal springs in the country since the time of the ancient Romans. Best explored on foot, magnificent examples of the city's Roman, medieval or Georgian heritage lie around almost every corner.

Since time immemorial, over half a million gallons of water a day at a constant temperature of 46°C have bubbled to the surface at this point. The ancient Celts believed the mysterious steaming spring was the domain of the goddess Sulis, and it is likely they were aware of its healing properties long before the arrival of the Roman legions in 43AD. However, the Romans were the first to enclose the spring, and within a few short years of their arrival, they had created the spectacular health resort known as Aquae Sulis, a name coined as a gesture to the Celtic population they now controlled. Indeed, they even dedicated the temple adjoining the baths to the joint goddess, Sulis-Minerva, to embody both the Celtic and Roman ideologies.

By the 3rd century, Bath had become so renowned that high-ranking soldiers and officials were coming here from all over the Roman world. Public buildings, such as a temple and forum, were added, and the whole city enclosed behind a stone wall. However, by the year 410, the Empire was crumbling and the last remaining legions were forced to return home. Aquae Sulis was abandoned, and within a few decades the drainage systems failed and the marsh returned.

Bath Abbey and Roman Baths

With the possible exception of Hadrian's Wall, the Roman remains at Bath are the most outstanding to survive in Britain. The main reason for their exceptional state of preservation is that for over a thousand years, they remained buried under several feet of dense alluvial mud. Ironically, the ancient baths remained hidden throughout the entire period of Bath's 18th-century renaissance as a spa town and were only rediscovered in the late 19th century; indeed, they were not fully excavated until the 1920s.

The restored remains which can be seen today are centred around the **Great Bath**, a rectangular lead-lined pool which is surrounded by steps and the truncated remains of a colonnaded quadrangle. Five separate phases were constructed over a 200-year period which began in the middle of the 1st century. The result is a superb complex of buildings incorporating swimming pools, mineral baths and a series of chambers heated by underfloor air ducts which would have functioned as saunas and Turkish baths. Open daily throughout the year, a visit to the Roman Baths includes admission to a fascinating museum of Roman coins, artefacts, jewellery, and perhaps the finest exhibit of all, a bronze head of the goddess Sulis Minerva.

The population of Bath fell away during the Dark Ages, and it wasn't until the 8th century that the Saxons founded a nunnery here which put the settlement back on the map. This was later elevated to monastic status when King Edgar of Wessex chose to be crowned *"King of all England"* here in 973. The present great church was begun in 1499 after its Norman predecessor had been destroyed by fire; however in 1539, Henry VIII's Dissolution of the Monasteries brought work to a halt. The church then had to remain without a roof for three quarters of a century, and indeed, the structure wasn't fully completed until 1901.

With its soaring buttresses, spiky ramparts and vast windows of clear glass, **Bath Abbey** is now considered the ultimate example of English Perpendicular church architecture. Its delicate stone fan-vaulting hangs 70ft above the nave, and its curious castellated tower is rectangular rather than square because it was built using the pillar-foundations of the earlier building. Inside, there is an unusual 18th-century portable oak font and a surprising number of monuments and tablets, more than in any church outside Westminster abbey. Some were erected in memory of the many wealthy invalids who flocked here in the 18th and early 19th centuries and were never well enough to return home.

One tablet in the abbey stands as a memorial to Richard *"Beau"* Nash, a legendary Bath figure who was one of the three people generally considered responsible for turning Bath into a fashionable Georgian spa town. Prior to Nash's arrival in the first decade of the 1700s, Bath had been a squalid community of around 2000 inhabitants whose former prosperity as a medieval wool town had all but disappeared. Historical accounts tell of farm animals roaming freely within the confines of the old Roman town and sewage running down the streets. Notwithstanding, small numbers of the rich and aristocratic continued to be attracted to Bath for its curative hot spring, and in the mid 17th century, the authorities finally took action to improve sanitary conditions, an initiative which was rewarded in 1702 by a visit from Queen Anne.

Nash, a man of great elegance and style, took on the job of improving the city. Despite having been something of a reprobate himself - he had been a modest failure at Oxford, in the Guards and as a lawyer, and only came to Bath in an attempt to earn his living as a gambler - he rose to become Bath's Master of Ceremonies, an unpaid, yet highly influential position to which he ascended when the previous MC was killed in a duel. He pressurised the corporation into paving, cleaning and lighting the streets, outlawed duelling and the wearing of swords, and set about creating a relaxed social atmosphere in which the gentry (the landed middle-class) could mix on equal terms with their social superiors, the aristocracy. Under his guidance, Bath became elegant and fashionable, and soon began to attract significant numbers of the *"right people"*, not only patrons, but also the architects and entrepreneurs who shared Nash's grand vision for the city.

Among these was the architect John Wood who, along with his son (also called John), designed most of the city's finest neoclassical squares and terraces. These included North and South Parades, Queen Square, The Circus, and most notably, Royal Crescent, John Wood the Younger's Palladian masterpiece which was the first terrace in Britain to be built to an elliptical design. Bath's third 18th-century founding father was Ralph Allen, an entrepreneur who made his first fortune developing an efficient postal system for the provinces, and who went on to make a second as the owner of the local quarries which supplied most of the honey-coloured Bath-stone to the city's Georgian building sites.

Situated in a splendid position adjacent to the Theatre Royal, **Popjoys Restaurant** is one of Bath's premier eating places. It is housed in the former home of Bath's legendary Master of Ceremonies, Richard *"Beau"* Nash, in a fine Georgian building which was constructed in the 1720s. Originally intended for the sole use of his

Popjoys Restaurant

lifelong mistress, Juliana Popjoy, Nash took up permanent residence himself after he lost his own house in a gambling game.

Today, Popjoys provides a stylish setting for an exceptional English-style lunch or dinner. Swiss proprietors Tomi and Nany Gretener pride themselves in serving unrivalled cuisine which is prepared using only the finest fresh local ingredients. The atmosphere too is superb, with elegant decor, stylish furnishings and service which is attentive yet unobtrusive. The dining area is split between the ground floor, which seats 36, and a dining/drawing room on the first floor, which seats 45. This magnificent first floor room has an open fireplace and its own bar, and can be reserved for private parties of ten or more. Popjoys Restaurant is open Mondays to Saturdays, from 12 noon to 2.30pm and 6pm till late, with last orders being taken at 11pm. *Popjoys Restaurant, Beau Nash House, Sawclose, Bath Tel: 01225 460494 Fax: 01225 465350*

A good place to begin a walk around central Bath is at the **Roman Baths**, whose adjoining **Pump Room** looks much as it did when it was completed in 1796. Now an elegant tearoom, a restorative cup of tea, coffee or spa water can be enjoyed here, often to the accompaniment of live chamber music. Items on show include two sedan chairs, one of which was used as a public taxi by the idle or infirm.

The abbey is situated almost adjacent the Pump Room, and a short distance away, the magnificent **Pulteney Bridge** spans the River Avon. The only example of the work of Robert Adam in Bath, it was inspired by Florence's Ponte Vecchio and is the only bridge in

Britain to incorporate a terrace of buildings. The nearby weir, with its graceful curving steps, is a superb example of Georgian refinement.

Set in beautiful gardens at the end of Great Pulteney Street only ten minutes' walk from Pulteney Bridge and the centre of the city, the Holburne Museum is a jewel in Bath City's crown and one of the finest examples of its elegant Georgian architecture. Originally a spa hotel, the building was adapted for the purposes of a museum by Sir Reginald Blomfield early in the 20th century to house the nucleus of the decorative and fine art collections of Sir William Holburne (1793-1874). On show can be seen superb examples of English and continental silver and porcelain, Italian maiolica and bronzes, together with glass, furniture, miniatures and paintings by such leading English and continental old masters as Gainsborough, Turner, Ramsay, Raeburn and Zoffany. The museum's collection has been added to over the years, with the emphasis remaining on work from the 17th and 18th centuries.

The *Crafts Study Centre* was founded at the *Holburne Museum* in 1977. This unique establishment incorporates an historic archive of reference books, working notes, documents and photographs relating to leading 20th-century artist-craftspeople, along with a permanent exhibition of their work. Items on display include woven and printed textiles, furniture, exquisite calligraphy and ceramics by such artist-potters as Bernard Leach, and also an important

Holburne Museum, Bath

collection of work on long-term loan from the Crafts Council. The museum organises a lively programme of events throughout the year, including lectures, concerts and special presentations. In addition, it mounts a series of temporary art and craft exhibitions on a variety of themes, including shows of work by leading contemporary artists and craftspeople. There is also an ongoing education programme, with study facilities being made available for individuals and groups by prior appointment, including access to the extensive library of archive material.

Visitors to the Holburne Museum can also enjoy a morning coffee, light lunch with a glass of wine, or afternoon tea with a homemade cake or pastry at the museum teahouse within the grounds. On fine days, customers can sit at tables outside and enjoy the beautiful garden. The museum is open from mid-February to mid-December, 11am to 5pm on weekdays and Bank Holidays and 2.30pm to 5.30pm on Sundays (closed Mondays until Easter), with free parking for museum and teahouse visitors. *Holburne Museum, Great Pulteney Street, Bath Tel: 01225 466669 Fax: 01225 333121*

Kennard Hotel

Staying at the **Kennard Hotel** provides the opportunity to discover and enjoy a true Georgian town house, now restored as a charming small hotel with its own unique character. Built in 1794 during the grand era of Bath's elegance and prosperity, all its thirteen bedrooms are thoughtfully and individually furnished for the comfort of guests. Each is equipped with a private bathroom, colour television, direct-dial telephone, hair dryer and tea/coffee making facilities, and some have the added luxury of a four-poster bed. A full choice of freshly-prepared English or continental breakfasts is served in the Kennard's garden-style bistro, a delightful room which has been refurbished from the original Georgian kitchen. Quietly situated close to peaceful Henrietta Park, the Kennard Hotel lies in an ideal city centre location, just over the famous Pulteney Bridge and only minutes level walk from the abbey and Roman baths. It is situated within easy reach of the station, and also enjoys easy access by road from Heathrow airport and London. AA selected and RAC acclaimed, the hotel is owned and personally-managed by the proprietors Malcolm Wright and Richard Ambler, and is an ideal touring base for exploring Bath, Wells and the beautiful rural countryside of the Cotswolds. *Kennard Hotel, 11 Henrietta Street, Bath Tel: 01225 310472 Fax: 01225 460054*

Moving to the north of the area once enclosed by Bath's Roman walls, Gay Street leads through Queen Square to The Circus, a striking example of neoclassical unity of design which is divided into three evenly-proportioned blocks of eleven houses. The street to the northeast leads to the National Trust-owned Assembly Rooms, one of the places polite 18th-century society used to congregate to dance, play cards or just be seen. The building was severely damaged during World War II and wasn't reopened until

Royal Crescent, Bath

1963. It is now leased to the Bath and North Somerset Council and incorporates an interesting Museum of Costume. (Open daily, 10am to 5pm, all year round.)

The street leading west from the Circus leads to **Royal Crescent**, a superb architectural set piece which is popularly regarded as the climax of Palladian achievement in this most classical of English cities. Built between 1767 and 1774 on a site which then overlooked unspoilt countryside, its huge sweep comprises thirty houses, each of which is divided by a giant Ionic half column. No. 1 Royal Crescent has been meticulously restored to its original Georgian splendour by the Bath Preservation Trust. Now designated a World Heritage Building, it is open on Tuesdays to Sundays, 10.30am to 5pm between 1 March and mid-December, with guided tours being available by arrangement.

Gainsborough Hotel

Those looking for accommodation in a quiet area of Bath within easy walking distance of all the main attractions should make a point of finding the **Gainsborough Hotel** in Weston Lane. Set within its own extensive grounds on the northwestern fringe of the city centre, this handsome detached Victorian residence lies within fifteen minutes walk of the Roman baths via the Royal Victoria Park.

The hotel is owned and personally-run by Richard Warwick, a genuinely welcoming host who, along with his helpful staff, will do everything in his power to ensure guests have a comfortable and enjoyable stay. The spacious and attractively furnished guest lounge enjoys a pleasant view of the lawned gardens, and there is also an intimate bar and two secluded sun terraces. The bedrooms are individually decorated and superbly equipped with en suite bath or shower-rooms, colour televisions, direct-dial telephones and a number of thoughtful extras.

Although car parking in Bath can often be a problem, the hotel offers free off-street parking for guests, who generally find it easier to walk into the city centre. Recommended by the AA and RAC, the Gainsborough Hotel is an English Tourist Board 3 crowns establishment. *Gainsborough Hotel, Weston Lane, Bath Tel: 01225 311380 Fax: 01225 447411*

Although the facades of Bath's Georgian houses were strictly controlled, the internal structure was left to the discretion of their individual owners, many of whom had very different ideas. The result is a fascinating jumble of contrasting masonry, narrow alleys, tradespeople's entrances and eccentric guttering - a half-hidden world which is well worth an inspection.

The old streets and buildings of Bath are said to be inhabited by an unusual number of ghosts. Two of the most infamous are the Grey Lady, whose characteristic jasmine scent has been detected around the **Theatre Royal** and nearby Garrick's Head inn, and the Black-hatted Man, who is said to appear in and around the Assembly Rooms. A guided Ghost Walk departs from the Garrick's Head each evening at 8pm during the summer months.

Bath contains an exceptional number of fine art galleries and specialist museums. The **Victoria Art Gallery** near Pulteney Bridge is the city's principal venue for major touring exhibitions. It also has a permanent collection of classical paintings and a smaller gallery displaying work from the area. (Open Mondays to Saturdays, 10am to 5.30pm, all year round; admission free.) The **British Folk Art Collection** (formerly the Museum of English Naive Art) in the Paragon is an absorbing anthology of 18th and 19th-century paintings which are characterised by their *"direct simplicity"*. (Open Tuesdays to Sundays, 10.30am (2pm Sundays) to 5pm between 1 April and 31 October.) On the same site is the Building of **Bath Museum**, a fascinating collection of models, drawings and illustrations which chronicle the city's unique architectural evolution. (Open Tuesdays to Sundays, 10.30am to 5pm, between 1 March and mid-December.)

The first recorded mailing of a Penny Black postage stamp was made in 1840 at No. 8 Broad Street, now the site of the **Bath Postal Museum**; exhibits include a reconstruction of a Victorian sorting office and a children's activity room. Open Mondays to Saturdays (also Sunday afternoons in summer), 11am to 5pm, all year round.)

Sally Lunn's House in North Parade Passage is thought to be the oldest house in Bath. Its cellar museum contains the kitchen used by the celebrated 17th-century cook who is attributed with inventing the Bath bun. (Open daily, 10am to 6pm, all year round.) The Bath Industrial Heritage Centre in Julian Road is a re-creation of an aerated water manufactory which provides an insight into one of the city's traditional industries. (Open daily, 10am to 5pm between Easter and 31 October; also weekends in winter.)

Sarnia Bed and Breakfast

An exceptional bed and breakfast establishment lying within easy reach of the centre of Bath, yet situated away from the bustle and congestion of the city, is ***Sarnia*** in Combe Park, Weston. Resident proprietors Jill and Rob Fradley provide the warmest of welcomes at their spacious Victorian home which has its own private parking and secluded garden.

The centrally-heated guest bedrooms are beautifully appointed, with colour TVs, tea/coffee making facilities, alarm clocks, and either an en suite or private bathroom. Guests are given the choice of a superb English, vegetarian or continental breakfast served in the bright and elegant dining room. Sarnia is English Touring Board 2 crowns highly-commended and rated 4 Qs by the AA, but is unsuitable for smokers. *Sarnia Bed and Breakfast, 19 Combe Park, Weston, Bath   Tel: 01225 424159*

Close to Weston on the northern edge of Bath, the ground rises onto Lansdown, a spur of downland which is the site of one the most remarkable follies in Britain. **Beckford's Tower** was built in the 1820s by the wealthy and eccentric scholar, William Beckford, to house his extensive art collection. Crowned by a lantern based on the Lysicrates monument in Athens, the pavilion and bell tower are a wonderful combination of Tuscan, Roman, Greek and Byzantine influences. Visitors climbing the 156 steps to the belvedere are rewarded with a magnificent view stretching from Wiltshire Downs in one direction to the Black Mountains of Wales in the other. There is also a small museum charting Beckford's extraordinary life in pictures, prints and models. (Open Saturdays, Sundays and Bank Holiday Mondays, 2pm to 5pm between early April and end-October.)

Those seeking first-rate bed and breakfast accommodation on the western side of Bath should make a point of finding **Cherry Tree Cottage** at Newton St Loe, a delightful former labourer's cottage which has been skilfully modernised and extended to form a very comfortable home from home. Situated in a conservation village on land owned by the Duchy of Cornwall, this charming establishment is conveniently located just a few miles from Bath and the A4 Bristol road, yet remains largely unspoilt by the march of time. Audrey Gay, a charming lady with a good sense of humour, offers accommodation in two very pleasant guest rooms which are ideal for overnight or longer stays. Her son and daughter-in-law are farmers in the village, so breakfast is an appetising affair prepared from fresh local produce. Unsuitable for smokers. *Cherry Tree Cottage, 37 Newton St Loe, Near Bath Tel: 01225 872768*

Another of Bath's follies, **Sham Castle**, was constructed on a hill to the east of the city by the quarry-owner Ralph Allen. Built to be seen from his town house, as its name suggests it is merely a romantic facade which is made even more picturesque by night-time illumination. Later in his career, Allen moved out to **Prior Park**, an ostentatious country mansion on the southeastern edge of Bath which now houses a co-educational school. Designed in classic Palladian style by John Wood the Elder, the house stands within impressive landscaped grounds whose ornamental lakes and superb neoclassical bridge were created under the guidance of Capability Brown and the poet Alexander Pope. The garden, which is currently undergoing a major restoration, enjoys magnificent views of the city and is open daily except Tuesdays.

The **Bath Tasburgh Hotel** is a delightfully-refurbished late-Victorian residence set in two acres of beautiful gardens on the eastern side of Bath. Conveniently situated on the A36 Warminster road just a mile from the many fine attractions of the city centre, it

The Bath Tasborough Hotel

overlooks the Kennet and Avon Canal and enjoys breathtaking views over the Avon Valley. The twelve guest bedrooms combine tasteful Victorian elegance with all the comforts of a good modern hotel. The four-poster, double and twin rooms all have bath or shower-rooms en suite, and are equipped with colour TVs, direct-dial telephones, radio-alarms, tea/coffee making facilities and a number of thoughtful extras. There is also an elegant drawing room and conservatory which are available to residents and their guests.

Fully licensed, the Tasburgh offers superb gourmet dinners by prior arrangement. Proprietors Susan and David Keeling are charming hosts who take great pride in providing the finest cuisine in beautifully-appointed surroundings. There is ample parking within the grounds, and guests are welcome to leave their cars at the hotel while exploring the delights of Bath. The hotel is just a short walk or bus ride from the centre and is ideal for short breaks, providing a comfortable place to relax after a hectic day's shopping or sightseeing. *Bath Tasburgh Hotel, Warminster Road, Bath Tel: 01225 425096 Fax: 01225 463842*

The National Trust owns 560 acres of countryside and woodland which together form the magnificent Bath Skyline Walk. Described in a leaflet obtainable from the National Trust shop in the abbey churchyard, the eight-mile footpath offers some spectacular views of Bath's Georgian outline. The route starts above Bathwick to the east of the city and also takes in an Iron Age fieldsystem.

Around Bath

Batheaston   Map 3 ref M4
2 miles NE of Bath on the A4

The A4 to the northeast of Bath leads to Batheaston, a dormitory village above and to the west of which lies **Little Solsbury Hill**. This 625ft flat-topped knoll is topped by a three-sided Iron Age hill fort, one of the simplest and earliest examples of its kind in the country. Excavations have shown that it was once encircled by a palisade, a sturdy fence made of wooden stakes driven into the ground which was built onto a low bank faced with dry stone walling.

Bathford   Map 3 ref N4
2 miles E of Bath on the A363

Another residential community which once belonged to Bath abbey, Bathford, is situated a mile to the southeast of Batheaston. Among the many fine 18th-century buildings to be seen here is **Eagle House**, a handsome residence which takes its name from the great stone eagle which stands with wings outstretched on the low-pitched gabled roof. At one time, the old redbrick paper mill by the river specialised in making paper for bank notes. The tall Italianate tower on the hill above Bathford is known as **Brown's Folly**. It was built following the Napoleonic Wars to provide local craftspeople with employment during the economic depression of the 1830s. The steep path leading up to the folly through Mountain Wood turns into an attractive nature trail along the way

Those travelling between Bathford and Bathampton on the opposite bank of the River Avon have to pay a small toll to cross the bridge. Although only a couple of miles from the centre of Bath, Bathampton's attractive grouping of canal, bridge, church and pub create their own distinct atmosphere. The last-named, the George, is a part 17th-century canalside inn which still has an external door in both its road and towpath sides. Viscount du Barry, the loser of the last legal duel to be fought in England (many illegal ones followed), was brought here following the ill-fated contest on nearby Bathampton Down. The unfortunate viscount died soon after and was buried in the nearby churchyard. According to local legend, however, his ghost has yet to be laid to rest and continues to haunt the inn.

Bathampton   Map 3 ref M4
1 mile E of Bath on the A36

Bathampton church is also the final resting place of Admiral Arthur Phillip, the first governor of New South Wales who took the initial shipload of convicts to the colony and established the settlement of Sydney. Considered by some to be the founder of modern Australia (although one would suspect the aboriginal population might not agree), a chapel in the south aisle which already contained memorials to the admiral's family was rechristened the *"Australian Chapel"* in the 1970s. Bathampton Down above the village is crowned by an ancient hill fort which, according to some historians, was the site of the 6th-century Battle of Badon in which the forces of King Arthur inflicted a crushing defeat on the Saxons.

Claverton   *Map 3 ref N4*
2 miles E of Bath on the A36

The ostentatious tomb of Ralph Allen, the quarry-owning co-founder of 18th-century Bath, lies in the churchyard at Claverton, a pleasant linear village lying on a loop off the A36, a mile to the southeast of Bathampton. The church itself is an unremarkable Victorian reconstruction whose most notable feature is a panel of 14th-century stained glass in the north transept. Six years before his death in 1764, Allen bought **Claverton Manor**, a 16th-century country mansion which was later demolished leaving only a series of overgrown terraces with impressive stonework balustrades. Some of the stone from the ruined house was used to construct the present manor on the hill above the village. The building was designed in elegant neoclassical style by Sir Jeffrey Wyatville, whose work is much in evidence at Windsor Castle, and is set in superb landscaped grounds.

Sir Winston Churchill is reputed to have made his first political speech at Claverton Manor in 1897; however, it is as a **Museum of American History** that the building is now best known. This

American Museum, Bath

17

absorbing museum was founded in 1961 by Americans Dallas Pratt and John Judkyn and is the only establishment of its kind outside the United States. The rooms have been furnished to show the gradual changes in American living styles, from the arrival of the Pilgrim Fathers in 17th-century New England to the Philadelphia and New York of the 18th and 19th centuries. The New Orleans room is like a set from *"Gone With The Wind"*, and there are scenes from the days of the Mississippi steamboats and the early Spanish colonisers of New Mexico. There is also a large section devoted to the history of the North American Indian and a display dedicated to the religious sect, the Shakers. (Open Tuesdays to Sundays, 2pm to 5pm between late-March and early-November.)

The narrow river valley between Bath and Bradford-on-Avon is shared by the A36, the main railway line and the Kennet and Avon Canal. For around two centuries, water has been mechanically transferred to the canal from the River Avon at the impressive **Claverton Pumping Station**. A mile further south, the canal makes a spectacular diversion over both river and railway by way of the **Dundas Aqueduct**, an impressive Bath-stone structure which is finished in characteristic neoclassical style.

Designed by the great engineer, John Rennie, the **Kennet and Avon Canal** was constructed between 1794 and 1810 to link the Thames with the Bristol Avon via Newbury and Devizes. A costly and ambitious project, much of its 75 mile length had to be cut through permeable rock which had to be lined with clay. The enterprise nevertheless succeeded in paying its investors a small dividend before the Great Western Railway arrived in 1841 to poach all its business.

In recent years, the Kennet and Avon Canal Trust has done much to restore this historic waterway, and it is now fully navigable between Bath and Caen Hill near Devizes. For those interested in joining a guided canal trip, narrowboats set out at regular intervals from Sydney Wharf and Bath's Top Lock. Alternatively, small electrically-powered self-drive boats are available from a variety of places including the Dundas Aqueduct.

Hinton Priory   *Map 3 ref M5*
4 miles S of Bath on the B3110

Two and a half miles south of the Dundas Aqueduct, the A36 passes close to the atmospheric ruins of **Hinton Priory**, an early Carthusian monastery which was founded in 1232 by Ela, Countess of Salisbury. As in other monastic houses belonging to this order, it was the practice for monks to occupy their own small dwellings which were set around the main cloister, often with tiny gardens attached. The community was generally known for its reclusiveness; however, one outspoken monk, Nicholas Hopkins, achieved notoriety in Tudor times as the confessor and spiritual adviser to 3rd Duke of Buckingham. As recounted by Shakespeare in Henry VIII, the so-called *"devil monk"* told Buckingham he would accede to the throne of England, an unfortunate prophecy which led to the Duke being executed and the monk being imprisoned in the Tower of London.

Several sections of the old priory remain, including the chapter house, with its library and dovecote above, the undercroft of the refectory, and parts of the guest quarters. (Open Wednesdays and Saturdays, 2pm to 6pm between early April and end-October.) One mile to the southwest, the church of **St John the Baptist** at Hinton Charterhouse predates the priory by a century or so. Although much altered, the font, south doorway and lower part of the tower survive from the original Norman structure.

Wellow
Map 3 ref M5

3 miles S of Bath off the A367

An undulating lane to the west of Hinton Charterhouse leads to the attractive village of Wellow. A stroll down the main street reveals some fine old houses, a raised walkway, and a charming circular dovecote which is believed to date from the 13th century. The part 14th-century church of St Julian contain a unique series of wall paintings dating from around 1500 depicting Christ and the twelve Apostles. On the southern edge of the village, the road descends steeply to a ford on the Wellow Brook, beside which stands a handsome medieval packhorse bridge and an old mill, now a private residence. Wellow is also the location of a first-rate pony trekking centre which offers a selection of rides for people of all ages and abilities.

One of the finest examples of a Neolithic long barrow in the west of England can be found beside the road to Shoscombe, three quarters of a mile to the southwest of Wellow. **Stoney Littleton** is a striking multi-chambered tomb which was originally constructed over 4000 years ago. Now restored, the interior can be inspected by obtaining a key from nearby Stoney Littleton Farm (a torch and old clothing advised).

Peasedown St John
Map 3 ref M5

5 miles SW of Bath on the A367

Continuing westwards across the A3062, the area incorporating PeasedownSt John and Radstock once stood at the heart of now almost-forgotten Somerset coalfield. Although coal from the margins of the Mendip hills had been extracted since the 1300s, it was during the 19th century that mining activities got underway in earnest. Indeed, the only building in Peasedown St John prior to 1817 had been the Red Post Inn, still a pleasant pub. The Braysdown colliery opened nearby in the 1820s and soon after, the deepest mine in the area was sunk at Camerton, a couple of miles to the west. Conditions underground were exceptionally hard. Miners often had to operate in seams which were only a couple of feet thick, their only equipment being a pick, a shovel, and a low sledge onto which the coal was loaded for removal. The coalfield began to decline after the First World War and the last colliery at Kilmersdon closed in the 1970s.

Visitors now have to look hard to find evidence of this once-thriving industry which at one time employed over 6000 people and produced over a million tons of coal a year. Some of now-landscaped spoil heaps can still be recognised as such, and there are also traces of the successive transport systems (canal, then tramway, then rival railways) which were constructed to take the newly-mined coal to market. In recent decades, the former mining communities, which include Paulton and Timsbury, have had to reinvent themselves as dormitory settlements for Bath and Bristol. Together they have little to offer the casual visitor, except for those with an interest in industrial archeology.

Midsomer Norton   *Map 2 ref L6*
8 miles SW of Bath on the A362

A memorial to the twelve miners killed in an accident at Wellsway coal works in 1839 can be found on the western edge of the St John the Baptist's churchyard in Midsomer Norton. According to the inscription, the men plummeted to their deaths as they were being lowered down the mine shaft when the rope holding the cage *"was generally supposed to have been maliciously cut."* A pleasant mixture of the old and new, Midsomer Norton's excellent shopping facilities blend attractively with its Georgian houses, 12th-century priory house, and late-medieval tithe barn, an imposing building which was converted into a Roman Catholic church in the early 20th century.

Although the history of the area is one of mining, with coal being hewn from nearby Norton Hill until as recently as the 1970s, it is hard to imagine that the beautiful surrounding countryside may once have been strewn with coal tips. Today, the sights and sounds of the colliery have been replaced by open farmland, wild flowers and bird song.

Centurion Hotel and Fosseway Country Club

Set in forty acres of parkland on the southern edge of Midsomer Norton, the family-run *Centurion Hotel and Fosseway Country Club* offers a superb range of facilities, both for leisure and for business. English Tourist Board 5 crowns commended, the luxuriousness of the hotel is reflected in the tastefully designed en suite bedrooms which are equipped with every modern amenity.

The restaurant offers a very high standard of English and continental cuisine from both a la carte and table d'hote menus, and the adjoining residents' lounge bar provides a delightful environment in which to relax. The hotel's three other bars also serve a range of freshly-prepared bar meals. Guests are welcome to use the heated indoor swimming pool, squash courts and recently created four-rink indoor bowling green, and there is also a well-established full-size outdoor bowling green set in most beautiful surroundings. The site also incorporates a lovely nine-hole parkland golf course which is a par 4 course, with green fees being payable at the hotel reception. Please enquire about the excellent value short breaks. *Centurion Hotel, Charlton Lane, Midsomer Norton, Near Bath Tel: 01761 417711 Fax: 01761 418357*

The interesting **Radstock and District Museum** is housed in a converted 18th-century barn at Haydon, a short distance from the Centurion Hotel. Devoted to the people of the North Somerset coalfield, it contains a unique collection of artefacts and photographs which tell the story of the local mines, railways, farms and schools. (Open Saturdays, Sundays and Bank Holiday Mondays, 2pm to 5pm, between January and November.)

Camerton
Map 3 ref L5

5 miles SW of Bath off the A367

As well as having contained the deepest mine in the area, the ancient community of Camerton has had a long and colourful history. The village stands beside the **Fosse Way**, the great Roman highway which linked the Channel coast near Exeter with the North Sea near Lincoln, and during the 400-year Roman occupation, the settlement was an important metal-smelting centre which produced pewter, bronze and iron for the Roman Empire. The site of the Roman settlement lay to the southwest of the present-day village, but has now completely disappeared.

In the early 19th century, the rector of Camerton was the well-meaning but tormented John Skinner, a man whose life was made a living hell by the conflicting demands of his children, his congregation, the local gentry, miners, mine owners, farmers and rival denominations. In his personal journal, all 98 volumes of which are now in the British Museum, he declared he *"would bear testimony that Camerton folk were as bad as the inhabitants of Sodom and Gomorrah."* Unable to stand it any longer, he eventually took his own life in the woods beside the rectory. During the 1950s, the local branch line, which is now long gone, was used for filming the classic Ealing comedy, The Titfield Thunderbolt. Lying in the lanes to the west of Camerton, the **Radford Farm and Shire Horse Stable** is an open farm which retains the traditional farming methods of the 1940s and 50s.

Priston
Map 3 ref M5

4 miles SW of Bath off the B3115

The church tower at Priston, a couple of miles to the north of Camerton, is crowned with a disproportionately-large weathercock which was presented to the parish by the local lord of the manor in 1813 as a flamboyant gift. **Priston Mill**, on the northern edge of the village, was given to the monks of Bath Abbey in 931 and has continued to supply flour to the people of the city ever since. Powered by a spectacular 25ft overshot water wheel, the millstones still produce genuine stoneground flour for retail sale. Visitors to the mill can learn about its operation and history, or take a trailer ride around the adjoining working farm. The site also incorporates an award-winning nature trail and adventure play area. (Open daily, 11am (2.15pm on weekdays) to 5pm between 1 April and 30 September.)

Farmborough
Map 3 ref L5

5 miles W of Bath off the A39

One of the finest eating places in the area can be found in the village of Farmborough, two miles to the west of Priston on the A39 Bath road. Taking the name of the community of which it forms part, **The Farmborough** is an impressive free house and restaurant which offers excellent hospitality and top quality food and drink. A handsome detached building standing in a lovely rural setting, its three and a half acre grounds provide ample parking for eighty cars.

The Farmborough

The exterior, with its half-timbered frontage, colourful window boxes, green striped window blinds and splendid entrance canopy, is attractive and welcoming, and the interior, with its comfortable seating and pleasant surroundings, makes dining here a very enjoyable experience. The first-class restaurant offers a selection of over sixty dishes and there is also a separate bistro menu, providing a choice to satisfy everyone. An extensive range of bar food is also served throughout the day, and for connoisseurs of fine beer there are six traditional ales. The Farmborough holds a full entertainments licence, and specialist marquee facilities are available for parties and wedding receptions. A popular eating place customers return to again and again, table reservations are advised. *The Farmborough, Bath Road, Farmborough, Near Bath Tel: 01761 470350*

Cameley   Map 2 ref L5
9 miles W of Bath off the A37

One of the most exceptional church interiors in the area can be found in Cameley, an attractive village which lies to the west of the A37 Bristol-Shepton Mallet road, four miles west of Camerton. The building was referred to by John Betjeman as *"Rip Van Winkle's Church"* because of the remarkable series of medieval wall paintings which lay undiscovered behind several centuries of whitewash until the 1960s. The murals are believed to have been painted between the 11th and 17th centuries and feature such diverse images as the foot of a giant St Christopher stepping through a fish and crab-infested river, a charming 14th-century jester complete with harlequin costume and belled cap, and a rare coat of arms of Charles I.

The two large artificial lakes lying in the northern foothills of the Mendips to the west of Cameley form an area which is sometimes referred to as the region's lake district. Originally constructed to supply Bristol with fresh water, they also provide a first-rate recreational amenity. The smaller **Blagdon Lake** was completed in 1899 and the **Chew Valley Lake** in 1956. Together they have around fifteen miles of shoreline and attract visitors from a wide area who come to fish, take part in watersports activities, or observe the wide variety of waterfowl and other birdlife which are attracted to this appealing habitat.

Chew Magna   Map 2 ref K5
10 miles W of Bath on the B3130

The former wool village of Chew Magna lies on the northern side of the Chew Valley Lake, four miles to the northwest of Cameley. This pleasant community contains some handsome Georgian houses, most of which are now owned by well-to-do Bristol commuters. The nucleus of the village is a three-sided green whose surrounding shops and pubs are linked by an unusual raised stone pavement. The striking early 16th-century church house at the top of the green once served as the village meeting house.

Beyond it, the impressive parish church of St Andrew stands as a testimony to Chew Magna's former wool-based prosperity. The interior contains a number of remarkable monuments, the most exceptional of which is the reclining wooden effigy of a knight, probably Sir John Hauteville, which shows him leaning on one elbow and resting his foot on a somewhat perplexed-looking lion. There is also an interesting double effigy of Sir John Loe, a 15th-century local squire who was reputed to be 7ft tall, and his wife, and another of the

Elizabethan sergeant-at-arms, Edward Baber and his wife, both of whom are sporting unusual double ruffs. Chew Court, a former summer palace of the bishops of Bath and Wells, lies behind a high wall adjacent to the churchyard.

Stanton Drew   Map 2 ref K5
9 miles W of Bath off the B3130

The ancient settlement of Stanton Drew lies to the south of the B3130, a mile and a half to the east of Chew Magna. A prehistoric site of some importance, the village stands beside a series of stone circles over half a mile across which were constructed by the Bronze Age Beaker People between 2000 and 1600 BC. The complex of standing stones consists of three stone circles, a lone stone known as **Hauteville's Quoit**, and a large chambered burial tomb known as **The Cove**. The stones are composed of three different rock types - limestone, sandstone and conglomerate - and are thought to have been erected for religious, or perhaps astronomical, purposes.

In common with many stone circles in the west of Britain, the origin of those at Stanton Drew are steeped in legend. The most widespread account tells of a foolhardy wedding party who wanted to continue dancing into the Sabbath. At midnight, the piper refused to carry on, prompting the infuriated bride to declare that if she had to, she'd get a piper from hell. At that point, another piper stepped forward to volunteer his services and the party resumed. But then the music began to get louder and louder and the tempo faster and faster, until the dancers were gripped in a furious jig they were powerless to stop. They realised too late that the good-natured piper was the Devil himself, and when his playing reached its terrifying climax, he turned them all to stone. To this day, this curious group of standing stones continues to be known as *"The Wedding"*.

The village of Stanton Drew also contains a number of noteworthy old buildings, many of which are listed. Among them is the 15th-century stone bridge over the River Chew, an unusual hexagonal thatched dwelling which later served as a turnpike toll-house, and an assortment of handsome 17th and 18th-century private residences.

A couple of miles to the north of Stanton Drew, the line of the ancient **Wansdyke** runs in a roughly east-west direction around the southern edge of Bristol. This great earthwork bank was built during the Dark Ages as a boundary line and defensive barrier against the Saxons. Although most evidence of its existence has long since disappeared, short sections can still be identified, for example along the ridge adjoining the Iron Age hill fort on Stantonbury Hill, east of Compton Dando, and at Maes Knoll, four miles further west.

CHAPTER TWO
Bristol & North Somerset

Blaise Hamlet, Henbury, Nr. Bristol

2
Bristol & North Somerset

Bristol

With a population of over 400,000 and a history dating back to the time of the Saxons, Bristol is a diverse regional capital which takes time to get to know. A good place for the visitor to begin is **Brandon Hill**, an area of open ground near the city centre which can be found to the west of the Park Street shopping area. Here, visitors can climb to the top of the **Cabot Tower**, a 100ft monument standing near the site of a chapel dedicated to St Brendan the Navigator which was erected in memory of another maritime pioneer, John Cabot. The first non-Scandinavian European to set foot on Newfoundland, Cabot's expedition of 1497 was financed by local merchants.

For centuries, Bristol was a major commercial seaport, and the magnificent view from the top of the tower reveals a complex series of docks and wharves along a curving stretch of water known as the **Floating Harbour**. This semi-artificial waterway was created when the course of the River Avon was diverted to the south early in the 19th century. A massive feat of civil engineering, the work took over five years to complete and was largely carried out by Napoleonic prisoners using only picks and shovels. Today, the main docks have moved downstream to Avonmouth and the Floating Harbour has become home to a wide assortment of recreational and smaller working craft.

Bristol was founded during Saxon times at the point where the curving River Frome joined the River Avon. This strategically-important bridging point at the head of the Avon gorge soon became a major port and market centre, and by the early 11th century, the town had its own mint and was trading with other ports throughout western England, Wales and Ireland. In 1067, the Normans began to build a massive stone keep on a site between the present-day Floating Harbour and Newgate, a place which is still known as **Castle Park** despite the almost total demolition of the structure at the end of the English Civil War. The heart of the old city lies to the west of here, around the point where Corn, Broad, Wine and High Streets converge.

Half a mile further west, **Bristol Cathedral** stands at the foot of Park Street on College Green. Founded in the 12th century as the great church of an Augustinian abbey, several original Norman features remain, including the southeast transept walls, chapter house, gatehouse, and east side of the abbey cloisters. Elsewhere there is some good 14th-century stained glass and a series of striking roof bosses in the north transept. Following the Dissolution of the Monasteries in 1539, Henry VIII took the unusual step of elevating the church to the status of cathedral, and soon after, the richly-carved choir stalls were added. This was followed over a century later by Grinling Gibbons' superbly carved organ case.

The structure wasn't fully completed until the 19th century when a new nave was built in sympathetic style to the existing choir. This now contains some exceptional monuments and tombs, along with a pair of unusual candlesticks which were donated in 1712 by the rescuers of Alexander Selkirk, the actual castaway on whom Daniel Defoe's character, Robinson Crusoe, was modelled.

Bristol Harbour

During the Middle Ages, Bristol expanded enormously as a trading centre and at one time it was second only to London as a seaport. This medieval trade was built on the export of raw wool and woollen cloth from the Mendip and Cotswold hills and the import of wines from Spain and southwest France. The city's first major wharf development was carried out at this time - the diverting of the River Frome from its original course into the wide artificial channel now known as *St Augustine's Reach*. A remarkable achievement for its day, the excavation created over 500 yards of new berthing and was crucial for Bristol's developing economy.

The city's increasingly wealthy merchants founded one of the most impressive parish churches in the west of England during this period. Originally set in a suburb to the east of the main channel, the church of St Mary Redcliffe is a wonderful arrangement of pinnacles, flying buttresses and sweeping stained-glass windows. Its soaring 290ft spire is a 19th-century addition to the original 13th-century tower, and its ornately decorated north porch was built to an unusual hexagonal design which is reputed to have been influenced by the architecture of China. An unusual roof boss in the shape of a circular maze can be seen in the north aisle. A giant replica of this, complete with water channels and raised walkways, can be seen in *Victoria Park*, half a mile away to the south. The sandstone beneath St Mary Redcliffe is riddled with underground passages known as the *Redcliffe Caves*. Interesting guided tours around these unusual natural caverns are conducted from time to time by the City Engineer's Department.

A stroll around Bristol city centre reveals an unusual number of interesting historic buildings. Queen Square, to the northwest of Redcliffe Bridge, is lined with handsome early 18th-century buildings, although two sides had to be rebuilt following their destruction in a riot in 1831. The *Theatre Royal* in King Street is the home of the acclaimed Bristol Old Vic theatre company. One of the oldest theatres in the country still in regular use, it was built in the 1760s with a semicircular auditorium, a rare feature for the time. Also in King Street, a striking timber-framed merchant's house of 1669 known as *Llandoger Trow* can be seen at its eastern end.

Continuing northwards into the area once contained within the city walls, The Exchange in Corn Street was built in the 1740s by the neoclassical architect, John Wood the Elder, whose work is much in evidence at Bath. The interior contains some fine detailing, including three heads symbolically depicting Asia, Africa and America which look down from above the doorways leading off the entrance hall.

The four low flat-topped pillars which can be seen outside the Exchange are known as *"nails"*. These are made of bronze and were used by local merchants to transact their business, giving rise to the saying, *"to pay on the nail"*.

The Red Lodge in Park Row contains the only remaining Tudor domestic interior in Bristol. Together with a similar residence called the White Lodge, it was built for Sir John Younge in the 16th-century. The building retains a remarkable number of original features, including one of the finest Tudor oak-panelled rooms in Wessex, and is now under the custodianship of the Bristol Museum and Art Gallery. (Open Tuesdays to Saturdays, 10am to 5pm, all year round.)

The elegant Georgian House in Great George Street was originally built in 1791 as a merchant's town house. Furnished in the style of the period, its contents have been selected from the permanent collection of the City Museum and Art Gallery, and include purchases made specifically for the house. (Open Tuesdays to Saturdays, 10am to 5pm, all year round.) The main City Museum and Art Gallery in Queen's Road occupies an imposing building at the top Park Street. Among its many fine exhibits is an exceptional collection of Chinese glass. (Open daily, 10am to 5pm, all year round.) Also worth seeing are John Cabot's House in Deanery Road and the Trinity Almshouses in Old Market Street to the east of the city centre. (Grounds open daily except Sundays, 10am to 4pm, all year round.)

The impressive **Melbournes Restaurant** can be found in Park Street, a short distance from the City Museum and Art Gallery. As one might guess from its name, this lively eating place offers a taste of Australian-style cooking as well as traditional European dishes. This former burger restaurant has come a very long way in the years since Tony and Nick took over. An ideal alternative to the usual run-of-the-mill eating place, the interior is beautifully decorated with Australiana of every description. There is seating for up to 100 people and most days the restaurant is packed with enthusiastic diners. While waiting to eat, why not try a Red Back beer - brewed in, and shipped directly from, Freemantle, Western Australia? Named after the poisonous redback spider, it packs quite a punch!

Just a quick glance at Melbourne's menu will start the taste buds tingling. The choice here is superb, with unusual starters like warm tartlet of broccoli, leeks with vegetarian cheese, or house-style gravadlax (smoked salmon marinated with fresh lime juice and fennel fern). Main courses include a fine selection of lamb, pork, game (in season) and chicken dishes, and the mouthwatering desserts

Melbournes

include profiteroles with cream and hot chocolate sauce. A standard of cuisine which is guaranteed to have you going back for more, Melbournes offers the opportunity to taste fine national cooking without the obvious stereotypes. The restaurant has a great atmosphere and is open every lunchtime and evening, except for dinner on Sunday and lunch on Monday. Advance booking recommended. *Melbournes, 74 Park St, Bristol Tel: 0117 922 6996*

Much of Bristol's waterfront has been now redeveloped for recreational use. **The Watershed Media Centre** on the western side of St Augustine's Reach is a modern arts complex with its own cinemas, galleries and harbourside cafe. The adjacent buildings have been converted to a first-rate exhibition centre. On the opposite bank, the Arnolfini Gallery specialises in exhibitions of contemporary visual art. It also has its own arts cinema, bookshop and stylish cafe-bar. (Open daily, 10am to 7pm, all year round; general admission free.)

Two impressive attractions lie across the swing bridge to the south of the Arnolfini Gallery: the **Lifeboat Museum** and the **Bristol Industrial Museum**. The latter houses a fascinating record of the achievements of the city's industrial pioneers, including those with such household names as Harvey (wines and sherries), Fry (chocolate), Wills (tobacco) and McAdam (road building). Visitors can find out about Bristol's history as a port, view the aircraft and aero engines made in the city since 1910, and inspect some of the many famous motor vehicles which have borne the Bristol name since Victorian times. During the summer, the museum offers interesting working demonstrations of some of its more spectacular exhibits. These a giant crane, steam railway, printing workshop and a variety of motor vessels. (Open Tuesdays to Sundays, 10am to 5pm, all year round.)

An excellent museum dedicated to the pioneering Victorian engineer, Isambard Kingdom Brunel, is located in the Great Train Shed at old Temple Meads station. The nearby *Exploratory* is a hands-on educational facility designed to put fun into everyday science. Situated in Gasferry Road on the southern side of the Floating Harbour, the *Maritime Heritage Centre* is an impressive visitor attraction which is dedicated to the history of Bristol shipbuilding. (Open daily, 10am to 6pm, all year round.) Among the increasing number of historic ships which line Bristol's wharves is Brunel's mighty *SS Great Britain*, the world's first iron-hulled, propeller-driven, ocean-going vessel which was built in the city in 1843. After a working life of 43 years, it was retired to the remote Falkland Islands where it was used as a storage hulk for over seventy years until 1970, when it was saved and brought back to the dry dock of its birth. Having now undergone a long and painstaking process of restoration, it is open daily, 10am to 5.30pm, all year round.

Brunel was also responsible for designing the *Clifton Suspension Bridge*, one of Bristol's most graceful landmarks which spans the Avon gorge a mile and a half to the west of the city centre. Opened five years after his death in 1864, it continues to carry an important route into the city. The bridge is suspended more than 200ft above the river and offers drivers and pedestrians a magnificent view over the city and surrounding landscape.

The National Trust-owned *Avon Gorge Nature Reserve* on the western side of the bridge offers some delightful walking through Leigh Woods to the summit of an Iron Age hill fort. A former snuff mill on the eastern side has been converted into an observatory whose attractions include a rare working example of a camera obscura. A nearby passage leads to the Giant's Cave, a subterranean chamber which opens onto a ledge high above the Avon.

Once a genteel suburb, modern Clifton is an attractive residential area whose elegant Georgian terraces are interspersed with stylish shops and restaurants. Clifton's *Goldney House*, now a university hall, is the location of a unique subterranean folly, *Goldney Grotto*, which dates from the 1730s.

Goldney Grotto, Bristol

A fantastic labyrinth filled with spectacular rock formations, foaming cascades and a marble statue of Neptune, its walls are covered with thousands of seashells and *"Bristol diamonds"*, fragments of a rare quartz found in nearby Avon Gorge. The grotto currently undergoing an ongoing programme of conservation and restoration, but is open most weekends between Easter and September. The renowned **Bristol Zoo Gardens** are located on the northwestern edge of Clifton in Clifton Down. (Open daily, 9am to 6pm, all year round.)

On the opposite side of the city, the former industrial centre of Keynsham lies in the sheltered valley of the River Avon, midway between Bristol and Bath. Now predominantly a dormitory town which thankfully is bypassed by the main A4, the settlement's present-day atmosphere belies its ancient roots. The area is known to have been populated by the Romans and indeed, the remains of two Roman villas were discovered here during excavations for a chocolate factory which have since been incorporated into an interesting small museum near the factory entrance.

In the late 12th century, an abbey was established in Keynsham on sloping ground near the River Chew. The piousness of the medieval monks, however, left much to be desired, and eventually they had to be banned from keeping sporting dogs, going out at night, employing private washer-women, and inviting female guests into the monastery. The abbey has long since disappeared, its only remaining outbuildings having been finally laid to rest beneath the bypass. However, the part 13th-century parish church has survived intact. A good example of Somerset Gothic, the interior contains some impressive monuments to members of the Bridges family. Two large brass mills were established in Keynsham during the town's 18th-century industrial heyday, one on the Avon and the other on the Chew. The former ceased production in the 1890s, and the latter in 1927, leaving behind some impressive industrial remains.

Around Bristol

Dundry   *Map 2 ref K4*
4 miles SW of Bristol off the A38
The attractive village of Dundry can be found on the southwestern outskirts of Bristol, between Maes Knoll and the A38 airport road. From its elevated position, the village offers superb views across the city. The magnificent four-tier church tower was funded by merchant venturers in the 15th century and was once used as a beacon for sailing ships in the Bristol Channel.

Dundry Inn

Situated opposite the church, the 290 year old **Dundry Inn** is a delightful pub and eating place which provides a warm traditional welcome. Hosts Graham and Maggie Hoyland have created a very friendly atmosphere where visitors can be sure of the finest hospitality. Along with a selection of fine local ales, they offer an impressive choice of food, from light snacks to appetising main meals, with a regular menu supplemented by a choice of daily specials. Recently restored and extended, this pleasant family-run inn is worth making a special effort to find. *Dundry Inn, Church Road, Dundry, Near Bristol Tel: 0117 964 1722*

Barrow Gurney
Map 2 ref K4

4 miles SW of Bristol off the A38

Prior to the building of the Blagdon and Chew Valley lakes, Bristol's fresh water came from the three small reservoirs at Barrow Gurney, a mile and a half to the west of Dundry. The first of these opened in 1852, but within two years it developed a leak and had to be drained, causing serious disruption to the city's water supply. The villages to the southwest of Bristol have undergone considerable change since the Second World War, many having now become little more than dormitory settlements for the city's commuters.

Congresbury
Map 2 ref J4

9 miles SW of Bristol on the A370

Congresbury, a sizable village which stands at the junction of the A370 and B3133 six miles to the southwest of Barrow Gurney, is no exception. However, its present-day character belies a long and eventful history which goes back to the days of the Romans. At that time, the settlement stood at the end of a spur of the Somerset marshes, and fragments of Roman and pre-Saxon pottery have been found on the site of the ancient hill fort which overlooks the present village.

The early Celtic missionary, St Congar, is believed to have founded an early wattle chapel at Congresbury in the 6th century. A tree bound by an iron hoop on the eastern side of the present-day church is still referred to as, *"St Congar's Walking Stick"*. This is reputed to have grown from the saint's staff which miraculously sprouted leaves after he had thrust it into the ground outside the chapel. Several centuries later, the Saxon King Ine heard of the wondrous occurrence and granted land for the founding of a stone church and monastery on the site, no trace of which remains today. Congresbury's present church is a spacious, part 13th-century structure with a soaring spire and a handsome Norman font which demonstrates some fine cable-carving.

The striking ecclesiastical-looking building which can be glimpsed through the trees from the churchyard is the part 15th-century vicarage. This was extended during the Regency period to create a curious architectural hybrid. Its distinct period styles now appear side by side, the medieval part serving as the church function room and the newer wing as the vicarage.

Puxton
Map 1 ref I4

10 miles SW of Bristol off the A370

The peaceful community of Puxton lies down a lane to the south of the

A370 Weston-Super-Mare road, two miles to the west of Congresbury. The village is worth a look for its eccentric church tower, which leans over at such an angle it looks as if it might topple at any minute causing its precarious-looking weathercock to nose dive into the churchyard. The church interior appears to have little changed since the main body of the building was rebuilt in the 1530s, a wonderful collection of high box pews, old wooden benches and later Jacobean fittings which include the pulpit, reading desk and altar rails.

Banwell   *Map 1 ref I5*
14 miles SW of Bristol on the A368

A narrow lane to the south of Puxton leads to Banwell, a pleasant settlement which once boasted a Saxon monastery. The village church has an impressive tower with a single turret and a striking interior with a fine rood screen and a Norman stone font. The latter is covered in unusual carvings and is topped by a curious pointed cover, both of which belong to later eras. The village also contains a substantial Victorian mansion known as **Banwell Castle**.

Court Farm Country Park on the northern edge of Banwell is an ideal place for an interesting and enjoyable day out, especially for those with young children. It can be found by following signs to Weston-Super-Mare from junction 21 on the M5, and then turning southeast onto the A371 towards Winscombe. As well as being a working farm, Court Farm offers a surprising array of outdoor and indoor attractions. The farm is home to an impressive variety of animals, including owls, ponies, shire horses, deer, pigs, sheep, goats and ducks, and younger visitors are encouraged to handle and bottle feed the many baby animals that are born here each year. They can

Court Farm Country Park

also enjoy free tractor rides around the site, see demonstrations of cows being milked, and play on the extensive grassy picnic areas.

Older visitors to Court Farm can also enjoy museums of rural life and informal tastings of farmhouse cider. There is also a pleasant gift shop and tearoom, and for those wishing to stray further afield, an attractive waymarked walk offers magnificent views over the surrounding countryside. Fascinating talks and displays of falconry are held throughout the year, along with a lively programme of special events. For details contact the farm. (Open daily, 10am to 5.30pm, all year round; closed Mondays, except Bank Holidays.) *Court Farm Country Park, Wolvershill Road, Banwell, Near Weston-Super-Mare Tel: 01934 822383*

In 1821, a remarkable series of caverns was discovered on Banwell Hill, above and to the west of the village. Known as the **Bone Caves**, they were found to discover the remains of prehistoric mammals, including bison, bear and reindeer. Some years later, the local bishop created an extravagant romantic park around the entrance to the caves which he filled with pyramids, monk's cells, fairy cottages and other fanciful buildings. The Avon Ski Centre and Mendip Riding Centre are two first-rate facilities which are located on the same site between the villages of Sandford and Churchill, a couple of miles to the east of Banwell.

The A371 to the west of Banwell skirts around the northern edge of the Bleadon Hills as it heads towards Weston-Super-Mare on the Bristol Channel coast. A couple of miles after crossing the M5, the road passes Weston Airport, home of the world's largest collection of helicopters and autogyros. The only museum in Britain dedicated to rotary wing aircraft, the **International Helicopter Museum** is a friendly volunteer-run establishment which has over forty exhibits ranging from single-seater autogyros to giant multi-seater helicopters. There are also displays on the history and development of these remarkable flying machines, a flight simulator, and a conservation hangar where aircraft are restored. (Open daily, 10am to 6pm, all year round.)

Weston-super-Mare   *Map 1 ref H5*
12 mile SW of Bristol on the A370

Weston-Super-Mare is a popular seaside resort which in recent years has developed as a centre of light industry. The town developed relatively belatedly as a seaside resort. In 1811, it was still a fishing hamlet with only 170 inhabitants; however, within the next 100 years it had grown to become the second largest town in Somerset and it now has a population of well over 50,000. Despite its relatively

Woodspring Museum, Weston-super-Mare

modern character, the locality has been inhabited since prehistoric times. The wooded promontory at the northern end of Weston Bay was the site of a sizable Iron Age hill settlement known as **Worlebury Camp**. In the 1st century AD, this was reputedly attacked and captured by the ancient Romans with great loss of life, an event confirmed by recent excavations which revealed a number of skeletons showing the effects of sword damage. A pleasant walk from the town now leads up through attractive woodland to the ancient hilltop site from where there is a magnificent view across the mouth of the Severn to Wales. Another spectacular view can be had from the clifftop site of the semi-ruined church at Uphill, a part-Norman structure which is situated at the southern end of Weston Bay, a couple of miles to the south.

Weston-Super-Mare has little of the grandiose architecture which characterises earlier seaside resorts such as Brighton or Torquay. Instead, it developed on a more comfortable scale with plenty of wide boulevards, leafy parks and open spaces. The town's greatest resource is its long safe sandy beach which is ideal for paddling, sunbathing and ball games. However, its gentle incline means that swimmers have to wade out a long way to find water deep enough to take the plunge.

Weston's early tourist development took place in the 1830s around the Knightstone, an islet joined to the shore at the northern end of Weston Bay onto which was eventually built a large theatre and swimming baths. Following the arrival of the railway in 1841, the town began its most rapid period of development and in 1867, a pier was built on the headland below Worlebury Camp which connected offshore Birnbeck Island with the mainland. Intended mainly as a berth for steamer traffic, it was found to be slightly off the tourist track and in due course, a more impressive pier was built nearer the town centre which, prior to serious fires in the 1930s and World War II, was approximately twice its present length.

Now, as then, the Grand Pier stands at the centre of an area crammed with souvenir shops, ice cream parlours, cafes and assorted attractions which are designed to appeal to the holidaymaker. Weston's indoor attractions include the Tropicana Leisure Complex and the Winter Gardens and Pavilion, both on the seafront, and the Heritage Centre in Wadham Street which is run by the Weston-Super-Mare Civic Society and offers free admission.

The **Woodspring Museum** in Burlington Street contains a series of fascinating displays on the social and natural history of the area, including the Victorian seaside holiday, royal potteries, early bicycles and period costume. It also incorporates an art gallery which offers a constantly changing programme of exhibitions. (Open Tuesdays to Sundays and Bank Holiday Mondays, 10am to 5pm, all year round.) Visitors can enjoy refreshments in the pleasant cobbled courtyard, and a guided Woodspring museum walk is also available on certain days between April and September. Situated adjacent to the museum, Clara's Cottage is a typical Victorian dwelling furnished in the style of 1900.

The narrow coast road to the north of Weston-Super-Mare passes along the beach at Sand Bay before terminating at Middle Hope, a high ridge jutting out into the Severn Channel whose western end, **Sand Point**, provides another fine viewpoint. The ridge overlooks a lonely salt marsh which is home to a wide variety of wading birds, including shelduck and oystercatchers. To the east, a path leads down to the Landmark Trust-owned **Woodspring Priory**, a surprisingly-intact medieval monastery which was founded around 1220 by a grandson of one of Thomas o Becket's murderers, William de Courtenay. The priory fell into disrepair following the Dissolution of the Monasteries of 1539 and its buildings were given over to agricultural use for many years. However, the church, tower, refectory and tithe barn have all survived, and the outline of the cloister can also be made out. (Open daily, 10am to 7pm (dusk in winter), all year round.)

Clevedon *Map 2 ref I3*
8 miles W of Bristol on the B3130

The impressive National Trust-owned **Clevedon Court** lies near junction 20 on the M5, five miles to the northeast of Woodspring Priory. One of the earliest surviving country houses in Britain, the main part dates from the early 14th century, and the tower and great hall are even older, dating from the 12th and 13th centuries respectively. Once partly fortified, this imposing manor house has been the home of the Elton family since 1709. Long-standing patrons of the arts, during the early 19th century they invited some of the finest poets and writers of their day to Clevedon Court, including Coleridge, Thackeray and Tennyson.

A few decades later, another member of the family invented a special technique for making the type of brightly-coloured pottery which became known as Eltonware. Particularly popular in the United States, many fine examples are now on display at the house, along with a collection of rare glass from the works at Nailsea. (Open Wednesdays, Thursdays, Sundays and Bank Holiday Mondays, 2pm to 5pm between late March and end-September.)

Clevedon Court

Clevedon Court is set within a delightful terraced garden which is known for its rare plants and shrubs. An attractive footpath leads up from here through nearby Clevedon Court Woods onto a ridge overlooking the Gordano valley. Clevedon Court is situated on the eastern edge of Clevedon, a genteel seaside town on the Severn estuary which has a population of around 20,000. A stylish holiday resort and residential centre since the late 18th century, at one time it was larger and more popular than Weston-Super-Mare. Its seafront is lined with bright stucco-fronted Regency and mid-Victorian houses in marked contrast to the grey limestone and brick of those further inland.

Although the town contains few of the popular attractions one would normally associate with a holiday resort, the exception is *Clevedon pier*, a remarkably slim and elegant structure which was built in the 1860s from iron rails which were intended for Brunel's ill-considered South Wales railway. When part of the pier collapsed in the 1970s, its long-term future was placed in jeopardy. During the 1980s, however, a major programme of restoration was begun which took around ten years to complete. Now open to the public once more,

Blaise Hamlet

throughout the summer the pier is used as a landing stage by large pleasure steamers such as the Balmoral and the Waverley, the only surviving seagoing paddle steamers in the world.

Among Clevedon's many fine old buildings is the **Market Hall** of 1869 which was built to provide a place for local market gardeners to sell their produce. The largely-Norman parish church of St Andrew contains some poignant memorials to local parishioners, many of whom died young. The Poet's Walk, a flower-lined footpath said to be popular with Victorian bards, begins at Clevedon promenade and leads up around Church and Wain's hills. The latter is topped by the remains of an Iron Age coastal fort and offers some magnificent views over the Severn estuary, the Levels, and the town itself. Clevedon's appeal continues to be romantic rather than dramatic. Its geographical position and lack of railway access prevented the large-scale development which so transformed other seaside resorts, and as a consequence it has managed to retain an atmosphere of tranquil refinement which still has a certain charm.

Walton-in-Gordano   *Map 2 ref I3*
8 miles W of Bristol on the B3124

To the northeast of Clevedon, two sweeping ridges of hills diverge like a great V. Between them lies the low Gordano valley, an area of former marshland dotted with settlements which incorporate the valley's name. Among them is Walton-in-Gordano, a small village containing an exceptionally beautiful four-acre garden, the **Manor House**, which is planted with rare shrubs, trees and herbaceous plants. (Open Wednesdays, Thursdays and occasional Sundays, 10am to 4pm between mid-April and mid-September.) To the southeast, the land rises sharply towards **Cadbury Camp**, an Iron Age hill fort situated in a dramatic position between the M5 and the village of Tickenham from where there is a fine view over the Levels to the Mendip hills.

Portishead   *Map 2 ref J3*
5 miles W of Bristol on the A369

The old coastal town of Portishead lies on the Severn estuary, four miles to the northeast of Clevedon. A resort whose early development had much in common with its near neighbour to the southwest, its customary villas, hotels, pier and bath houses (or saltings) began appearing in the 1820s and 30s. The town's character changed abruptly in 1867, however, when the railway arrived to transform it into a busy port and industrial centre. A number of seaside attractions nevertheless remained, although these were largely redirected towards the cheaper end of the market. Today, Portishead is a flourishing residential centre whose finest features are its part 14th-century parish church, the Court, a handsome Tudor residence with an unusual polygonal tower, and Portishead Point, an impressive wooded viewpoint overlooking the Severn estuary.

A visit to Portishead's **Brackenwood Garden Centre and Woodland Gardens** offers a truly enjoyable day out. Situated on the coast road to the west of Portishead town centre, this delightful eight-acre woodland garden has been developed over the past thirty years by the current owners, Jenny and John Maycock. A stroll through the grounds at any time of the year reveals a spectacular display of colour, with many rare and beautiful specimen trees, plants and flowering shrubs. Initially planted with rhododendrons and camellias, the gardens now incorporate a bluebell wood, bog garden, azalea bank and wildlife pool. There is also a waterfowl enclosure which is home to a collection of rare ducks, swans and geese. An inspiring setting, visitors can enjoy breathtaking views across the Bristol Channel to the distant hills of South Wales.

The Brackenwood Garden Centre

The Brackenwood Garden Centre also offers numerous ideas for the garden. The centre offers a superb range of shrubs, trees and herbaceous plants, and as growers, it is well placed to provide the soundest advice. Qualified staff are always on hand to offer guidance in selecting plants and seedlings that are best suited to the customer's individual requirements. There is also a large display   of gift and craft ideas, departments specialising in floristry and silk flowers, and a renowned restaurant and tearoom seating around 100 which offers a constantly changing menu of daily hot specials, delicious snacks and cream teas. *Brackenwood Garden Centre, 131 Nore Road, Portishead, Near Bristol Tel: 01275 843484*

The area to the northeast of Portishead around the mouth of the Bristol Avon is one which generally should be avoided by the casual visitor. Substantial modern dock facilities have been constructed on either side of the river to handle today's ocean-going cargo ships which are too gigantic to make it through the narrow Avon gorge to Bristol. Avonmouth, on the northern bank, is a place of heavy industrial activity which may inspire a certain awe when viewed from the M5 Avon Bridge.

Henbury
Map 2 ref K2
4 miles NW of Bristol on the A4018

A couple of noteworthy places of interest can be found on the northwestern approaches to Bristol. The modern suburb of Henbury contains the remarkable Georgian oasis of **Blaise Hamlet**, a collection of nine detached stone cottages which were designed in romantic rustic style by John Nash in 1809. Each was built to a different design for the retired estate workers of the nearby Blaise Estate. The cottages themselves are not open to the public, although visitors enjoy free access to the village green. An interesting museum of everyday life is housed in nearby **Blaise Castle House**, a late 18th-century mansion set within 400 acres of parkland which once formed the nucleus of the estate. Displays include toys, costumes and household equipment. (Open Tuesdays to Sundays and Bank Holiday Mondays, 10am to 5pm, all year round; admission free.)

Also in Henbury is **Vine House**, a two-acre landscaped garden incorporating a delightful water garden which contains an impressive collection of trees and flowering shrubs. (Open at selected times under the National Gardens Scheme.)

Westbury on Trym
Map 2 ref K2
2 miles NW of Bristol on the A38

Nearby Westbury-on-Trym is the location of the National Trust-owned **Westbury College Gatehouse**, the 15th-century gatehouse of a now-demolished ecclesiastical college. (Open by arrangement with the local vicar.)

CHAPTER THREE
Eastern Mendips

Chewton Cheese Dairy

3
Eastern Mendips

Frome

Standing beside the river from which it takes its name, the ancient settlement of Frome is the largest centre of population in northeast Somerset. The parish church of St John the Baptist was founded as a Saxon monastic house by St Aldhelm in the 7th century, and by the time of the Norman invasion, Frome was already a sizable market town which extended from the river to the church on the hill above.

The Frome valley became an important centre of the wool industry during the late Middle Ages when a series of weirs was constructed to regulate the flow of water to the many water-powered weaving and fulling mills which lined the riverbank. (Fulling was a process which softened and increased the volume of woven cloth by immersing it in water and feeding it through a series of mechanically-driven rollers.) However, the industry largely collapsed in the 18th century when textile production transferred to the industrial North, although one mill, A H Tucker's, continued in production right up until the 1960s.

The prolonged decline of the textile industry meant that little of central Frome was redeveloped during the 19th and early 20th centuries, and as a result, many of its narrow medieval streets and alleyways have survived intact. Some have wonderful names like Pudding Bag Lane and Twattle Alley, and others, such as Gentle Street, the steeply-sloping Catherine Hill, and Cheap Street with its water course running down the centre, are highly impressive in their own right. The bridge over the River Frome incorporates an 18th-century lockup gaol, near to which can be seen the famous Bluecoat School and the recently-restored *Blue House*, an elegant almshouse dating from 1726.

Best explored on foot, the centre of Frome is an attractive conservation area which contains an unusual number of interesting shops, cafes and residential buildings. Lively markets continue to be held in the town every Wednesday and Saturday, and for those interested in local history, there is an excellent museum which is open Wednesdays, Fridays and Saturdays between early March and late November. There is also an interesting arts and crafts complex, the **Black Swan Centre**, situated in Bridge Street.

Around Frome

Beckington   *Map 3 ref N6*
4 miles NE of Frome off the A36

To the north of Frome, the river winds its way towards its confluence with the Bristol Avon. Three miles downstream, the former wool village of Beckington boasts one of the largest and most ornate Norman church towers in Somerset, with the rest of the building being predominantly 15th-century Perpendicular. The village contains the remains of a medieval castle and some fine stone-built houses, including the early-Georgian **Cedars**, a former ecclesiastical hospital known as the Abbey, and Seymour's Court, a farmhouse once owned by Sir Thomas Seymour, the ambitious Lord High Admiral who married Henry VIII's widow, Catherine Parr.

Lullington   *Map 3 ref N6*
4 miles NE of Frome off the A36

The peaceful community of Lullington lies on the opposite bank of the river, a mile and a half to the southwest of Beckington. The Norman village church is worth a look for its remarkable carved north doorway - a striking combination of arched lintels and twisted columns crowned by a mysterious seated figure. A gateway on the southern edge of the village marks the start of the footpath to **Orchardleigh Park**, an imposing Victorian pile which was built in the 1850s. The lake in the grounds has an island in its western corner on which is perched a small church whose churchyard contains the grave of Sir Henry Newbolt, the author of Drake's Drum, who died in 1938. (Open at certain times.)

Rode   *Map 3 ref N6*
5 miles NE of Frome off the A361

Situated between the A36 and A361 a mile to the north of Beckington, the pretty village of Rode is the location of the famous **Rode Bird Gardens**. This impressive seventeen-acre park is home to around 1200 tropical birds, many of which are allowed to fly freely. The grounds incorporate a miniature woodland steam railway, a pets' corner, and a series of lakes inhabited by flamingos, penguins and many other species of birds and waterfowl. There is also an ambitious captive breeding programme dedicated to the rearing of rare and endangered species. (Open daily, 10am to 6pm, all year round.)

Norton St Phillips
Map 3 ref M5
6 miles N of Frome on the A366

One of the finest medieval inns in Britain can be found in Norton St Philip, a lovely old village which lies a couple of miles to the northwest of Rode near the junction of the A366 and B3110 Bath road. The splendid *George Inn* was founded as a house of hospitality in the 13th century by the monks of nearby Hinton Priory, the second-oldest Carthusian monastery in the country. The timber-framed upper floors were added in the 15th century when the inn doubled as a warehouse for storing locally-produced woollen cloth. In 1668, the diarist Samuel Pepys stayed here with his family while on his way to Bath, recording the experience simply as, *"Dined well. 10 shillings."*

A decade and a half later, the ill-fated Duke of Monmouth made the George his temporary headquarters shortly before the Battle of Sedgemoor in 1685. According to local legend, nine local men implicated in the ill-fated uprising were imprisoned here after the battle in what is now the Dungeon Bar. Later they were taken away and burnt at the stake in a nearby orchard. Virtually unaltered since, the present-day inn is a wonderful fusion of medieval stonework, oriel windows and timber-framing. There is also a superb courtyard and minstrels' gallery at the rear.

A former wool village which once stood on the main Bath to Salisbury road, Norton St Philip also contains some fine 17th-century stone cottages and a handsome mainly-Perpendicular church. St Philip's was rebuilt in the 17th century and is believed to contain the grave of the Siamese-twin sisters who were born in the nearby hamlet of Foxcote. Sadly now lost, their tombstone is reputed to have been carved with a likeness of the girls who had *"two bodies upward and one stomach."*

Farleigh Hungerford
Map 3 ref N5
6 miles NE of Frome on the A366

The old fortified settlement of Farleigh Hungerford lies on the A366 Radstock to Trowbridge road, two miles to the northeast of Norton St Philip. The village is worth visiting for the impressive remains of *Farleigh Castle*, a medieval fortification which stands on a rise above the River Frome to the northeast of the centre. The structure was built by Sir Thomas Hungerford, the first Speaker of the House of Commons, on the site of an old manor house which he acquired in the late 14th-century. According to local lore, Sir Thomas failed to obtain proper permission from the Crown for his fortifications, an oversight which almost led to his downfall. However, the Hungerfords were a powerful family who owned land throughout Wiltshire, and so he was able to pacify the situation and survive the king's displeasure.

A century and a half later, another member of the Hungerford family was less successful in avoiding royal disfavour. After having imprisoned his wife in one of the castle towers for four years, he was eventually executed by Henry VII for *"treason and unnatural vice."* The castle then changed hands in the early 18th century; however, the new owners saw the structure more as a stone quarry than a place to live and proceeded to remove most of its walls to build a new Gothic-style mansion on the opposite side of the village. Nevertheless, an impressive shell of towers and perimeter walls has survived intact, along with the castle **Chapel of St Leonard's**. This contains a striking 15th-century mural of St George, some fine stained glass and a number of interesting monuments, including the tomb of Sir Thomas Hungerford himself. Farleigh Castle was brought under the ownership of English Heritage early in the 20th century and is now open daily, 9.30am (2pm on Sundays) to 6.30pm (4pm in winter), all year round.

Nunney   *Map 3 ref M7*
3 miles SW of Frome off the A361

Another fortification with an interesting history can be found at Nunney, a picturesque community which lies in the lanes to the north of the A361 Shepton Mallet road, three miles to the southwest of Frome. The focus of this small former market town is its dramatic moated castle which was begun in 1373 by Sir John de la Mare on his return from the French wars. Thought to be modelled on the Bastille, the structure consists of four solidly-built towers which stand on an island formed by a stream on one side and a broad water-filled moat on the other. The castle came under Parliamentarian artillery fire during the English Civil War and, despite having a garrison of only one officer, eight men and a handful of civilian refugees, held out for two days. The bombardment, however, damaged the building beyond repair and it had to be abandoned, leaving the romantic remains which can be seen today.

One of the thirty-pound cannonballs which helped to demolish the castle walls is on view in Nunney's 13th-century All Saints' church. Reached via a footbridge over the moat and another over a small stream, this much-altered building also contains an interesting model of the castle in its original condition, as well as a number of tombs to the de la Mare family, including an impressive stone effigy of Sir John. Nunney's old Market Place, which was granted a trading licence by the Crown in 1260, is also worth a visit. A mile to the north of Nunney, the road to Mells passes through the attractive village of Whatley, the location of an interesting vineyard and herb garden which is open to the public on Wednesdays to Sundays, 10am to 6pm between 1 April and 30 September.

Mells
Map 3 ref M6

3 miles NW of Frome off the A362

Mells must be one of the loveliest villages in northeast Somerset. Once the easternmost limit of the lands belonging to the mighty Glastonbury Abbey, Abbot Selwood drew up plans to rebuild the village in the shape of a St Anthony's cross (a cross with four arms of equal length) in the 15th century. Only one, New Street, was completed and this architectural gem can be seen to the south of St Andrew's parish church. The church itself is a magnificent example of Somerset Perpendicular, with a soaring 104ft tower and spectacular pinnacled south porch. The interior contains a remarkable collection of monuments designed by some of the 20th-century's most acclaimed artists, including Lutyens, Gill, Munnings and Burne-Jones. One is to Raymond Asquith, the eldest son of the Liberal Prime Minister, Herbert Asquith, who was killed during the First World War. A memorial to the pacifist and antiwar poet Siegfried Sassoon can be seen in the churchyard.

According to legend, the Abbot of Glastonbury, in an attempt to stave off Henry VIII's Dissolution of the Monasteries, dispatched his steward, John Horner, to London with a gift for the King consisting of a pie into which was baked the title deeds of twelve ecclesiastical manor houses. Far from persuading Henry, however, Horner returned to Somerset the rightful owner of three of the manors himself - Mells, Nunney and Leigh-upon-Mendip - for which he paid of total of £2000. This remarkable act of disloyalty is commemorated in the nursery rhyme Little Jack Horner which describes how Jack *"put in his thumb and pulled out a plum"*, i.e. the deeds to the property. The manor house at Mells, which is not open to the public, remained in the hands of the Horner family until the early 20th century when it passed to the Asquiths by marriage.

Hidden in the lanes to the northwest of Mells, the 18th-century country mansion, **Babington House**, stands at the end of a striking avenue of beech trees, a mile from the A362 Frome to Radstock road. Dating from around 1700, with a wing of 1790, the house and nearby church of St Margaret form an elegant composition. The church, with its original timber panelling and box pews, is a rarity in Somerset having been left virtually unchanged since it was constructed in 1750. These two buildings are the only evidence of the medieval hamlet of Babington, a settlement which suffered as a result the 18th-century fashion for emparking, that is, removing the dwellings of the local inhabitants in order to create an uninterrupted view of the landscaped grounds from the big house.

Shepton Mallet

An important centre of communications since pre-Roman times, the old market town of Shepton Mallet lies on the River Sheppey, a little to the west of the Fosse Way, the old Roman route which at this point comprises a stretch of the modern A37. The settlement's Saxon name, which means simply *"sheep town"*, reveals its main commercial activity during the pre-Norman and medieval periods, originally as a centre of wool production, and later as a weaving town. The industry reached its peak in the 15th century and it was then that Shepton Mallet's magnificent parish church was constructed. This striking building has one of the earliest Perpendicular towers in the county and a remarkable wagon roof with some 350 carved oak panels and around 300 bosses, each fashioned to a different design.

Perhaps Shepton Mallet's most characteristic structure, however, is its 50ft **Market Cross**. Built around 1500 and restored in 1841, it has been the town's civic and commercial hub for almost 500 years. Indeed, a lively modern market continues to be held here every Friday. Several participants in the Duke of Monmouth's ill-fated Pitchfork Rebellion were executed at the market cross in 1685 on the orders of the infamous Judge Jeffreys. The curious roofed structure standing nearby is a fixed market stall dating from the 15th century which is the only surviving remnant of Shepton's medieval butchers' market, or shambles. A lane running east off Town Street leads past the church to the old prison. Thought to be well away from the threat of enemy bombs, the Domesday Book was brought here for safe keeping during the Second World War.

Tucked away in Leg Square in a quiet corner of Shepton Mallet, the **Kings Arms** is an obvious favourite with local people, some of whom still refer to it as the *"Dust Hole"* from the early days it was frequented by employees from the local quarry. At least four centuries old, this handsome old inn has been altered and extended on several occasions over the years. Along with a fine selection of real ales and beers, the Kings Arms offers an impressive choice of dishes

The Kings Arms

which are served each day until 9pm. Children are welcome and the extensive menu includes a special list of attractively-named dishes for younger diners. There's an excellent family atmosphere and adults can join in the fun with a game at the pool table or skittle alley. The inn also has an attractive function room available for wedding receptions and special occasions, and for those looking for comfortable overnight accommodation, there are three very pleasant en suite guest rooms. *Kings Arms, Leg Square, Shepton Mallet, Somerset Tel: 01794 343781*

Present-day Shepton Mallet is a prosperous light industrial town which has a good selection of shopping and leisure facilities. One of its largest industrial employers is Showerings, the makers of Babycham. For those with an interest in the town's social and industrial past, it is well worth visiting the district museum at the top of the High Street. Each year, Shepton Mallet plays host to two well-established agricultural shows: the **Mid-Somerset Show**, which is held in the town on a Saturday in August, and the **Royal Bath and West Show**, which is held over four days at the end of May on a permanent site beside the A371, a couple of miles to the south of the town centre.

Around Shepton Mallet

Leigh-upon-Mendip   *Map 7 ref L7*
4 miles NE of Shepton Mallet off the A367

A lane to the south of Babington House leads to Leigh-upon-Mendip (pronounced lye), a sizable village whose church tower is modelled on its sister church at Mells. The interior, however, is less ornate, with a plain Norman font and simple pews. The eastern terminus of the **East Somerset Railway** lies to the south of the A361 Frome to

Shepton Mallet road, three miles to the southwest of Leigh-upon-Mendip. Originally a broad gauge line dating from the 1850s, the present steam railway was founded by the wildlife artist, David Shepherd, in 1975. Assisted by an enthusiastic team of volunteers, Shepherd has assembled an outstanding collection of steam locomotives, varying in size from the tiny Lord Fisher to the mighty Black Prince. An impressive replica Victorian engine shed and workshop has been built at West Cranmore where there is also a railway museum, art gallery and restaurant. (Open Wednesdays to Sundays (weekends only in winter months), 10am to 5.30pm between March and December.)

Doulting
Map 7 ref L7

1 mile E of Shepton Mallet on the A361

Lying on the A361 a mile and a half to the west of West Cranmore, the village of Doulting is unusual in Somerset in that its church has a tall spire, rather than a tower. An imposing part 12th century building with a handsome exterior, it also has a splendid two-storey porch which incorporates a curious carving of the green man into its vaulting; the church interior, however, is over-restored and disappointing. The village dates back to the 8th century when King Ine of Wessex gave the local estate to Glastonbury Abbey after his nephew, St Aldhelm, the Abbot of Malmesbury and first Bishop of Sherborne, died here in 709. The saint's body was carried back to Malmesbury along a circuitous route which was marked for posterity by a series of tall stone crosses. The church, a statue, and the spring in the former vicarage garden are all dedicated to St Aldhelm. The spring was later incorporated into a holy well which became a place of pilgrimage during the Middle Ages.

The 15th-century **Tithe Barn** at the southern end of the village is a relic of Doulting's monastic past. This great building was constructed to store tithes, one tenth of the local tenant farmers' crops which they paid annually to their ecclesiastical landlords. Another important source of revenue came from the great quarry which lay to the north of the village. The fine cream-coloured stone from here was used in the construction of Wells cathedral and for later additions to Glastonbury abbey. The handsome terrace of estate-style cottages near the church is more recent, however, dating from the end of the Victorian era.

The renowned **Waggon and Horses** at Doulting Beacon is a superb 18th-century inn and restaurant which was once a stop on the coaching route between London and Taunton. A listed building of architectural and historical interest, it has a lovely exterior and an atmosphere which is quite unique. Joint owners Francisco Cardona and Richard Pajan are both blessed with great artistic flair. Not only is Vienna-born Richard is acclaimed for his inventive cooking, and in particular for his dishes from Central Europe and the Mediterranean, but he is also known for his ability as a fine artist. Indeed, the inn incorporates an exhibition of work by locally-based artists and includes a selection of paintings and drawings by Richard which are shown in an upstairs gallery. This is also the location of a Steinway grand piano - Francisco's most treasured possession. For as Richard possesses an artist's talent, so Francisco is a most accomplished pianist.

Waggon and Horses

Customers at the Waggon and Horses represent a wide cross-section of the population, from local farmers, artists and craftspeople, to Wells cathedral music teachers and BBC journalists. Many come to hear the regular classical music concerts that are held here - yes, concerts in a pub! Recently, a recital was held by Phillip Fowke, a pianist of international repute, who declared the Royal Albert Hall and the Waggon and Horses to be his two favourite venues.

The inn also has an attractive walled garden containing rare and exotic breeds of domestic fowl. A special favourite with children, it is also an ideal setting for barbecues which are a regular feature of summer weekends. Amongst his other talents, Francisco is a keen horseman and breeder who spends all the time he can spare with his four-legged friends. For those visiting the area, a visit to the Waggon and Horses provides an unforgettable gastronomic and artistic experience. *Waggon and Horses, Doulting Beacon, Near Shepton Mallet, Somerset   Tel: 01749 880302*

Downside

Map 3 ref L7

1 mile N of Shepton Mallett on the A37

Situated on the main A37 half a mile to the northeast of Shepton Mallet, the **Downside Inn** in the hamlet of Downside is a pleasant country pub which is ideally placed for the motorist taking a leisurely drive down to the South West. Well thought of locally, good food and drink is available here at all times. A selection of traditional ales, lagers, wines and spirits is served in the two comfortable bars, and there is also a family room where children are welcome.

Downside Inn

The inn offers an extensive range of home-cooked meals, grills and snacks, as well as a traditional roast lunch on Sundays. The menu is reasonably priced and take-away food is also available - a welcome bonus for the traveller. The Downside Inn caters for private functions, business meetings and wedding receptions, and its attractive gardens, with their tropical bird aviaries, are an ideal place to spend a relaxing hour or two, perhaps enjoying a summer barbecue. *Downside Inn, Downside, Shepton Mallet, Somerset Tel: 01749 342129*

To the north of Shepton Mallet, the Fosse Way ascends into the eastern margins of the Mendip Hills as the A37, before turning northeastwards and becoming the A367 Bath road.

Oakhill

Map 3 ref L7

2 miles N of Shepton Mallet on the A367

The old brewing village of Oakhill lies in the lanes to the north of this junction. Although the original brewery has long since disappeared, in recent years a new one has opened to provide the pubs and inns of the district with traditional ales. This is also the location of *Oakhill Manor*, a small country mansion set in an attractive 45-acre estate which has been developed as a popular visitor attraction. The car park is connected to the house by a scenic miniature railway which incorporates a scaled-down version of Cheddar Gorge, and the manor itself contains an extraordinary collection of models and pictures, mostly relating to historic forms of land, sea and air transport. (Open daily between Easter and late-October.)

Stratton-on-the-Fosse

Map 3 ref L6

5 miles N of Shepton Mallet on the A367

Three miles to the northeast of Oakhill, the A367 passes through Stratton-on-the-Fosse, a former coal-mining community which is also the home of the famous Roman Catholic boys' public school, *Downside Abbey*. The school occupies the site of a monastery which was founded in 1814 by a group of English Benedictines who had emigrated to France but were subsequently driven out by the French Revolution. The steady expansion of the school during the 20th century encouraged the monks to move to a new site on higher ground near the existing abbey church, an impressive building which took over seventy years to complete and numbered among its architects, Sir Giles Gilbert Scott.

Stratton-on-the Fosse also possesses a handsome parish church which stands on the opposite side of the A367. This striking part medieval building incorporates a number of 18th and 19th-century features which were added at the time the local coal mining industry was at its peak. Hard to imagine today, Stratton is situated at the southern edge of the once prosperous, but now almost forgotten, Somerset coalfield. The last mine in the town was closed in 1968.

The impressive *Red House Holiday Homes* can be found off the A367 Shepton Mallet to Bath road on the edge of Stratton-on-the-Fosse. These attractive stone holiday cottages have been converted from former farm buildings to offer excellent, largely ground-level accommodation. Quietly situated and set well back from the road, they are neatly planned, with open views and plenty of easy parking. The interiors are furnished to a high standard and everything is provided for a comfortable stay. The on-site farm shop is able to

Red House Holiday Homes

satisfy most everyday requirements, and Proprietor Val Creed is on hand at seemingly all hours to offer help and deal with her guests' enquiries. With the Cheddar Gorge and many other attractions nearby, the Red House Holiday Homes provide an excellent base for touring in this attractive area. *Red House Holiday Homes, Red House Farm, Stratton-on-the-Fosse, Near Bath, Somerset Tel: 01761 412319 Fax: 01761 417478*

Chewton Mendip
Map 2 ref K6

5 miles N of Shepton Mallet on the A39

One of the most celebrated cheese makers in the North Somerset can be found at Chewton Mendip, a village lying on the A39 Wells to Bath road, four miles to the west of Stratton-on-the-Fosse. **Chewton Cheese Dairy** at Priory Farm is one of the few remaining cheese-making dairies which still uses truly traditional methods. Here, the ancient art of preparing genuine Cheddar cheese can be observed at first hand. The fascinating process gets underway with milk pasteurisation at around 7.30am and continues throughout the day until the cheese is put into the press around 3pm. Taking anything up to eighteen months to mature at carefully regulated temperatures, the length of ageing is what gives the cheese its distinctive thick rind. Visitors can call at the dairy at any time of day, though there are usually not many around for the 7.30am start. There is also a licensed restaurant serving coffees, lunches and cream teas, and a shop where Cheddar cheese and a range of other dairy produce can be purchased, together with cider, wines and preserves. There is even a secluded caravan park on the estate which provides an

Chewton Cheese Dairy

excellent base for touring the area, details of which can be obtained from Priory Farm. *Chewton Cheese Dairy, Priory Farm, Chewton Mendip, Somerset   Tel: 01761 241666 Fax: 01761 241202*

Croscombe   Map 6 ref K7

1 mile W of Shepton Mallet on the A371

The former weaving village of Croscombe lies a couple of miles to the west of Shepton Mallet beside the A371 Wells road. Among the many fine stone buildings to be found here is the parish church, an imposing part 13th-century building with a tall spire, a rarity in Somerset. The interior contains a magnificent collection of Jacobean dark oak fittings carved in a variety of heraldic and pastoral designs. The medieval manor house behind the church has recently been restored by the Landmark Trust.

For those looking for a pleasant country pub offering good food, fine ales and first-rate accommodation, the **Bull Terrier** at Croscombe has it all. Standing on the A371 midway between Shepton Mallet and Wells, this charming inn offers the warmest of welcomes to visitors and locals alike. The atmosphere inside is warm and inviting, with wood-panelled walls and attractive traditional furnishings. In addition to a good variety of real ales, Ruth and Barry Vidler serve an impressive choice of freshly-prepared bar meals, both at lunchtimes and in the evening. They also provide comfortable accommodation in three well-appointed guest rooms, two of which have en suite facilities. *Bull Terrier, Croscombe, Near Wells, Somerset Tel: 01749 34365*

Bull Terrier

Evercreech *Map 7 ref L8*

3 miles SE of Shepton Mallet off the B3081

A church tower which is much more characteristic of the county can be found at Evercreech, an attractive village which lies on the B3081 Bruton road, a mile to the southeast of the Royal Bath and West showground. The impressive Perpendicular tower of St Peter's, with its multi-tiering, complex tracery and tall pinnacles, creates an impression of great height. Perhaps the most striking feature of the church interior is the ceiling of the nave, which is adorned with sixteen painted angels and a series of gilded roof bosses. The church overlooks a delightful square with a village cross which is surrounded by some lovely old stone cottages and almshouses.

A real gem of an inn can be found just to the south of the showground on the main A371 Shepton Mallet to Castle Cary road. **The Pecking Mill Inn** and Hotel is a handsome 16th-century pub and eating place which enjoys magnificent views over open countryside to the Mendip Hills. Since taking over in 1983, resident proprietors Bryan and Janice Challoner have built up a reputation for providing delightful food, drink and hospitality. With its oak-beamed restaurant, interesting bar, open log fires and blue lias stone-walling, the atmosphere of the inn is traditional and welcoming. The restaurant has seating for 36 diners and offers an extensive a la carte menu,

The Pecking Mill Inn

while lighter meals are served in the bar. Rated 3 crowns by the English Tourist Board, the hotel has a private breakfast room and residents' lounge, along with six well-presented en suite guest rooms which are equipped with excellent modern facilities. *Pecking Mill Inn, Evercreech, Near Shepton Mallet, Somerset Tel: 01749 830336 Fax: 01749 831316*

Evercreech Junction   *Map 6 ref L8*
3 miles SE of Shepton Mallett on the A371

Situated to the west of Evercreech on the main A371 Shepton Mallet to Castle Cary road, the **Natterjack Inn** at Evercreech Junction is a truly superb establishment which offers the very best in food, ales

Natterjack Inn

and hospitality. The building was originally called the Railway Hotel, but after the Beeching cuts it was poignantly renamed the Silent Whistle; some time later it was changed again to its present name. Hosts Richard and Nicky have successfully built up an enviable reputation at this impressive pub and eating place.

All their food is freshly-prepared using the finest local ingredients and offered at very modest prices. Diners can choose from a selection of delicious steaks and sauces from the griddle, ranging from a tasty 8oz prime fillet to an enormous 32oz prime Scotch rump. There is also a wide range of homemade specials, hot bites and delicious fish dishes, with a special choice for vegetarians and under 12s. Booking is advised, as this friendly inn is very popular at meal times. *Natterjack Inn, Evercreech Junction, Near Shepton Mallet, Somerset Tel: 01749 860253*

Batcombe *Map 7 ref L8*

4 miles SE of Shepton Mallet off the A359

A lane to the east of Evercreech leads through the hamlet of Stony Stratton to Batcombe, a secluded community set within an Area of Outstanding Natural Beauty. The village, whose name means *"Bata's valley"* in Saxon, has one of the finest perpendicular Gothic church towers in Somerset. This was built in the 16th-century when Batcombe was an important centre of the wool industry. Indeed, at that time the district's nine cloth mills were producing more woven material than those along the River Avon between Bath and Bristol.

In these days of rush and push, pressure and schedules, many people look forward to a restful holiday in a peaceful haven. Such a place is **Batcombe Vale House**, the beautiful home of Donald and Mary Sage which is situated in a neighbouring valley within a

Batcombe Vale House and Campsite

conservation area surrounded by trees, lakes and wild landscaped gardens. The only sounds to be heard here are the song of blackbirds, the plop of fish, and the munching of cows. The grounds incorporate a small campsite with thirty individual pitches, all with hard road access, electric hookups, and water, drainage and rubbish points. Listed among the AA's best campsites, its excellent facilities are located in an attractive log cabin and include showers with free hot water, toilets, payphone and tourist information. First-rate bed and breakfast accommodation is also available at the house, where the three lovely guest rooms look out across the private lakeside garden onto beautiful countryside.

The 120-acre area surrounding the campsite is part of Batcombe Vale, an idyllic setting where guests may wander and picnic in the fields. The valley incorporates three lakes which are filled with tench, rudd and carp, some up to 20lbs in weight, and there are also rowing boats for the more energetic. A keen local historian with a wealth of knowledge of the district, Donald is always willing to answer visitors' questions. He is also happy to provide footpath maps for those wishing to attempt any of the one to ten-mile walks through the surrounding hills. There are several excellent inns en route to supply midday and evening meals, most notably the award-winning Batcombe Inn, and for those touring the area by car, the many places of interest lying within a fifteen mile radius include Stourhead Gardens, Longleat, Wells and Yeovilton Air Museum. *Batcombe Vale House and Campsite, Batcombe, Near Shepton Mallet, Somerset Tel: 01749 830246*

East Pennard
Map 6 ref K8

3 miles S of Shepton Mallet off the A37

A lane to the west of Evercreech leads across the A371 and A37 to the secluded village of East Pennard, the location of one of Britain's few organic wine producers. The *Avalon Vineyard* produces an attractive range of wines, ciders and mead, all from organically-grown produce. (Open daily, 2pm to 6pm between 1 June and 31 August.) The sheltered south-facing slopes of the southern Mendips have become popular with the new generation of English vine growers, most of which welcome visitors for tours and wine tastings.

Pilton
Map 6 ref K7

1 mile SW of Shepton Mallet off the A361

A fine example can be found at Pilton, a scattered village which lies just off the A361 Shepton Mallet to Glastonbury road, two miles to the north of East Pennard. The extensive grounds of *Pilton Manor*, a former summer residence of the bishops of Glastonbury, have been planted with vines, mostly of the German Riesling variety, and visitors are invited to stroll around the estate and sample the end product. The present manor house is a curious combination of architectural styles: largely Georgian, its central Venetian-style window is surrounded by medieval-looking turrets, pinnacles and castellations.

Another legacy from the abbey is Pilton's great cruciform tithe barn which stands on a hill surrounded by beech and chestnut trees. Sadly, its magnificent arch-braced roof was destroyed when the building was struck by lightning in 1963. The roof of the parish church of St John has been more fortunate: considered a 15th-century masterpiece, it has survived for over 500 years. This superb little building also has an impressive Norman south doorway with characteristic zigzag carving, some fine 15th-century stained-glass in the chancel, and a unique collection of early instruments which were used to provide the congregation with musical accompaniment prior to the arrival of the church organ.

North Wootton

Map 6 ref K7

4 miles W of Shepton Mallet off the A361

A lane to the northwest of Pilton leads to the village of North Wootton, home of the prize-winning **Wootton Vineyard**. Here, the Gillespie family produce a range of estate-bottled white wines which are available to sample and purchase. (Open Mondays to Saturdays, 10am to 5pm, all year round.)

Greenacres Camping

North Wootton is also the location of **Greenacres Camping**, an award-winning family-owned campsite which is set in four and a half acres of beautiful Somerset countryside. Licensed for only thirty tents, trailer-tents or motor-homes, there is never any overcrowding at this spacious, flat and easily accessible site. Younger visitors have access to an attractive play area with swings and slides, and there are also daily tractor rides to provide extra amusement. Campers are welcome to use the fridges and freezers at the house, and the nearby village has a large pub which serves excellent bar and restaurant meals. First-rate bed and breakfast accommodation is also available at the owners' lovely bungalow where the beautiful guest rooms are furnished to a high level of comfort. Greenacres has excellent facilities and was recently named *"Campsite of the Year"* by Camping And Walking magazine. (Unsuitable for dogs.) *Greenacres Camping, Barrow Lane, North Wootton, Near Shepton Mallet, Somerset   Tel: 01749 890497*

West Pennard   *Map 6 ref K8*
4 miles SW of Shepton Mallet on the A361

Back on the main A361 Shepton Mallet to Glastonbury road, the village of West Pennard is the location of a small National Trust-owned property, the **West Pennard Court Barn**. This unusual five-bay barn dates from the 15th-century and can be found in the lanes to the south of the village. (Open by acquiring the key from nearby Court Barn Farm; admission free.)

CHAPTER FOUR
Central Somerset

Glastonbury Abbey

\

4
Central Somerset

Glastonbury

The ancient ecclesiastical centre of Glastonbury, a small town with an immense history, is a mecca for those encompassing such diverse beliefs as paganism, Christianity, Arthurian legend and the existence of UFOs. Before the surrounding Somerset Levels were drained in the 18th century, the dramatic form of **Glastonbury Tor** stood out above a great expanse of mist-covered marshland. Known throughout the region as the Isle of Avalon, one of the first outsiders to sail up the River Brue and land at this distinctive conical hill was the early Christian trader, Joseph of Arimathea, who arrived from the Holy Land around 60 AD. According to local legend, Joseph was walking one day on nearby Wearyall Hill when he plunged his staff into the ground. Miraculously, the stick took root and burst into leaf, and this he took as a sign he should found a church. A wattle and daub structure was duly erected at the spot which later became the site of the great **Glastonbury Abbey**.

Joseph's staff is reputed to have grown into the celebrated Christmas-flowering Glastonbury hawthorn, and although the original is believed to have been felled during Cromwellian times by an overzealous Puritan (he was blinded by a flying shard of wood in the process, no doubt as a gesture of retribution), one of its windswept ancestors can still be seen on the crest of Wearyall Hill. In an extended version of the legend, Joseph was accompanied on one of his visits to Glastonbury by his nephew, the young Jesus Christ, an occurrence which is reputed to have provided William Blake with the inspiration for his hymn, Jerusalem.

Glastonbury Tor remains a landmark which can be seen from miles around, although curiously, it is often less conspicuous when viewed from close by. The 520ft hill has been inhabited since

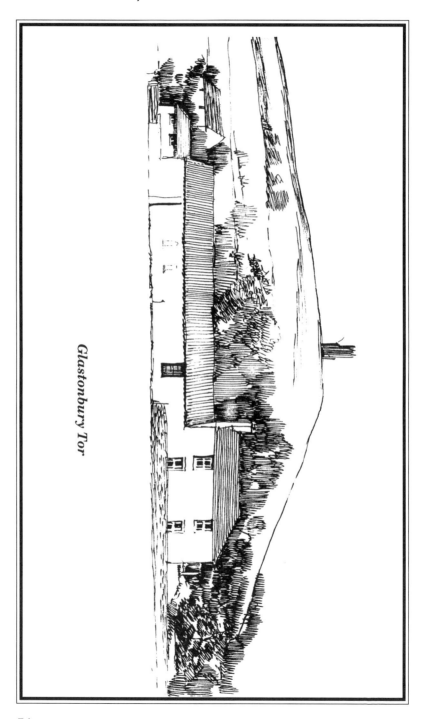

Glastonbury Tor

prehistoric times, and excavations on the site have uncovered evidence of Celtic, Roman and pre-Saxon occupation. Because of its unusually regular shape, it has long been associated with myth and legend. For example, in its time it has been identified as the Land of the Dead, the Celtic Otherworld, a Druid's temple, magic mountain, Arthurian hill-fort, ley line intersection, and rendezvous point for passing UFOs.

Along with mystical energy, the tor offers a magnificent panorama across Somerset to Wells, the Mendips, the Quantocks and the Bristol Channel. The view from the top is most breathtaking on a misty day when the tor is surrounded by a sea of silver cloud. The striking tower at the summit is all that remains of the 15th-century **Church of St Michael**, an offshoot of Glastonbury Abbey which fell into disrepair following the Dissolution of the Monasteries in 1539. In that turbulent year, the tor became a place of execution when the last abbot of Glastonbury, Richard Whiting, and two of his monks were hanged near the summit for opposing the will of Henry VIII.

The wooded rise standing between Glastonbury Tor and the town centre is known as **Chalice Hill**. During one of his visits in the 1st century AD, Joseph of Arimathea is supposed to have buried the Holy Grail (the cup used by Christ at the Last Supper) beneath a spring which emerges from the foot of the hill's southern slope. The spring forms a natural well which was partially enclosed within a masonry structure during medieval times. This is now situated in an attractive garden maintained by the **Chalice Well Trust**. The spring water has a high iron content which leaves a curious rust-coloured (some say blood-coloured) residue in its wake. It is also reputed to have curative powers and flows at a constant rate of 25,000 gallons per day into a pool known as the Pilgrim's Bath. (Garden open daily, 10am to 6pm between early-March and end-October; 1pm to 3pm in winter.)

The dramatic remains of **Glastonbury Abbey** can be found to the northwest of Chalice Hill in the heart of old Glastonbury. If the legend of Joseph of Arimathea is to be believed, this is the site of the earliest Christian foundation in the British Isles. The abbey is thought to have been founded by King Ine around 700 AD, and under St Dunstan, the 10th-century abbot who went on to become the Archbishop of Canterbury, it grew in influence so that by the time of the Norman invasion, it owned estates covering an eighth of the county of Somerset. The abbey continued to grow under the guidance of the Benedictines until a disastrous fire destroyed most of the abbey buildings in 1184.

Glastonbury Abbey

When the foundations of the replacement great church were being excavated seven years later, a wooden sarcophagus was discovered 16ft down between the shafts of two ancient crosses. Inside were found the bones of a large man and a slender woman, and one story tells of how the woman's long golden hair seemed in a perfect state of preservation until a monk touched it, transforming it to dust. A lead cross found nearby convinced the abbot that he had discovered the remains of King Arthur and Queen Guinevere, although it was known at the time that this was the burial place of at least three kings from the later, Saxon period.

The abbot's discovery could well be described as timely, given his pressing need for funds to pay for the abbey's reconstruction. Notwithstanding, Glastonbury soon became an important place of pilgrimage, and when the main part of the abbey had been completed in 1278, King Edward himself arrived to witness the final re-interring of Arthur's bones in a magnificent new tomb in the choir. The regenerated great church was a massive 560ft in length, with a splendid central bell-tower, twin west towers, a unique clock, and a series of shrines to the great and the good.

The abbey continued to wield considerable power until Henry VIII's Dissolution of the Monasteries of 1539 forced it to close. The building was abandoned and soon fell into disrepair: its walls were plundered for building stone and Arthur's tomb was destroyed. A number of impressive remains have nevertheless survived, the best-preserved being **St Mary's Chapel**, the shell of the great church, and the 14th-century **Abbot's Kitchen**. The last named is a charming structure with a vaulted roof and a fireplace in each corner which has survived almost intact. The old abbey gatehouse now houses an interesting small museum whose exhibits include a selection of historic artefacts from the site and a model of the abbey as it was at the time of the Dissolution. (Open daily, 9.30am to 6pm (or dusk if earlier), all year round.)

The abbey's principal **Tithe Barn** stands on its own to the southeast of the main monastic buildings. Although it is relatively small for such a great estate, it incorporates some fine sculptured detail, notably the carved heads on the corner buttresses and emblems of the four Evangelists on the gables. The barn is now the home of the **Somerset Rural Life Museum**, an imaginatively-presented exhibition dedicated to the era of pre-mechanised farming. As well as a collection of historic farm implements, there are special displays devoted to cider making, willow shoot (or withy) cutting, peat digging and thatching. (Open daily, 10am (2pm Sundays) to 5pm, all year round.)

Abbey Tea Rooms and Restaurant

The delightful ***Abbey Tea Rooms and Restaurant*** is situated in the heart of Glastonbury adjacent to the town centre and Abbey ruins. Spotlessly clean and well-patronised by visitors and locals alike, customers come from miles around to enjoy the superb, freshly-prepared home-cooked food. The establishment is owned and personally-managed by Mary Parker, a charming hostess who makes a point of greeting each customer individually. A variety of snacks and light meals are served throughout the day, accompanied by a choice of fourteen varieties of tea and six of coffee. Delicious cream teas are available at most times, along with the superb selection of homemade cakes for which the tearoom is renowned. A rarity in this era of fast food, the linen table cloths and fresh flowers are a delight to behold. Mary Parker and her staff also serve an excellent dinner menu from 7pm on Fridays and Saturdays and a special lunch on Sundays. *Abbey Tea Rooms and Restaurant, 16 Magdalene Street, Glastonbury, Somerset   Tel: 01485 832852*

During the Middle Ages, Glastonbury Abbey was an internationally renowned centre of learning which attracted scholars and pilgrims from all over Christendom. Such were the eventual numbers that a guesthouse had to be built outside the abbey walls. Originally constructed around 1475, the much ornamented George and Pilgrims Hotel can still be seen in the High Street near the Market Cross. The old timber beams of this striking building are adorned with carved angels and the fireplace in the bar is surrounded by Delft tiles which are over two centuries old. The interior is guarded by a series of curious monks' death masks, and at one time, the building was even rumoured to have a subterranean passage leading from the cellar into the abbey grounds.

A couple of doors away, ***The Tribunal*** is a handsome early 15th-century courthouse which now houses the tourist information office. The two square panels above the doorway each contain the royal emblem of the Tudors, an indication that the king's justice was meted out inside. Among the many fine churches to be found in Glastonbury are ***St John's Baptist church*** in the High Street, which has an imposing 134ft tower, and St Mary's Roman Catholic church in Magdalene Street, which dates from the outbreak of the Second World War.

A National Trust footpath to the east of Glastonbury leads to ***Gog and Magog***, the ancient oaks of Avalon. This famous pair of living antiquities are all that remain of an avenue of oaks which, sadly, was cut down in the 1900s to make way for a farm. One of the felled trees was eleven feet in diameter and was recorded as having over 2000 season rings.

Set amidst delightfully tranquil and unspoilt countryside a couple of miles to the east of Glastonbury, the Old Oaks Touring Park offers excellent amenities and wonderful views of the Mendip Hills. This impressive family-owned caravan and camping park is run by Jim and Sally White, friendly hosts who have developed it over more than a decade. Specially tailored for touring caravans, the spacious grass and hard pitches are divided by hedges, trees and shrubs, and almost all have electrical hookups.

Old Oaks Touring Park

An ideal family park with plenty of space for outdoor games, other attractions include a play area with swings, an indoor games room and a heated swimming pool. The excellent amenities include a heated fully-tiled toilet and shower block, baby care room, disabled unit, bathroom, laundry and dish-washing facilities. The park shop stocks most day-to-day requirements, and the adjoining tourist information section has details of the area's many visitor attractions. Voted *"Best Campsite in Southern England"* by the AA in 1995 and 1996, the park has received many other awards and accolades. *Old Oaks Touring Park, Wick Farm, Wick, Near Glastonbury, Somerset Tel: 01458 831437*

Another historic place of interest can be found to the northwest of Glastonbury town centre in a field beside the road to Godney. This was the site of a prehistoric **Lake Village** which was discovered in

1892 when it was noticed that a section of an otherwise level site was studded with irregular mounds. Thought to date from around 150 BC, the dwellings were built on a series of tall platforms which raised them above the surrounding marshland. An interesting collection of artefacts recovered from the site can be seen in the town museum.

In its time, Glastonbury has been called the Ancient Avalon, the New Jerusalem, and the *"Holyest Erthe"* in England. It is a place of natural enchantment which attracts an ever-growing number of pilgrims of the new age who are drawn by its unique landscape, atmosphere and quality of light.

One of the greatest mysteries of the locality, indeed one which may possess something of a credibility gap, is difficult to observe except from the air. Much loved and eagerly propounded by those with an interest in astrology, the **Glastonbury Zodiac** was brought to light in 1935 by Katherine Maltwood when she was researching a book on the Holy Grail. According to Maltwood, the twelve signs of the zodiac appear in their correct order as recognisable features of the landscape, their outlines being delineated by streams, tracks, ridges and ancient boundaries. The entire formation lies within a circle with a seven mile radius whose centre lies three miles to the south of Glastonbury near the village of Butleigh. Its origins remain a subject of speculation.

Glastonbury to Bridgewater

Meare   Map 6 ref J7
3 miles NW of Glastonbury on the B3151

The attractive village of Meare lies three miles along the B3151 Wedmore road to the northwest of Glastonbury. When approaching the village from the east, an unusual medieval building known as the **Abbot's Fish House** can be seen on the northern side of the main road. Prior to about 1700, this isolated structure stood on the edge of **Meare Pool**, a substantial lake over a mile and a half in diameter which provided Glastonbury abbey with a regular supply of freshwater fish. Before the lake was drained, this plain, early 14th-century building was used for storing fishing equipment and salting fish. It has three ground-floor and two first-floor rooms, the upper level being reached by way of an external staircase.

Rising to only 30ft above sea level, the surrounding Somerset Levels cover an extensive area bordered by the Mendips to the northeast, the Quantocks to the west, and Ham-stone country to the south. For thousands of years, this low-lying stretch of countryside spent much of the year submerged under a layer of standing water, conditions ideal for the formation of peat, which is created when a lack of oxygen prevents the normal decomposition of vegetation. Piecemeal channels had been dug for centuries, but it was only in the last quarter of the 18th century that a coordinated drainage system was proposed which included the construction of the great **King's Sedgemoor Drain** of 1794. As a result, the Levels are now crisscrossed by a complex system of artificial waterways which, in ascending order of size, are known as ditches, rhines (pronounced reens) and drains. This fascinating area contains a rich diversity of wildlife and has much to offer the walker, bird-watcher, rural historian and casual visitor.

Westhay
Map 6 ref I7

4 miles NW of Glastonbury on the B3151

At Westhay, a mile and a half to the west of Meare, the **Peat Moor Visitor Centre** offers a fascinating insight into the history and ecology of the Somerset Levels. A series of imaginatively-presented displays describe the development of commercial peat-digging through the ages, the special trades which have grown up in this unique environment, and the measures which have been taken to conserve the area's flora and fauna. There is also a reconstruction of a section of the oldest manmade walkway in the world, the *"Sweet Track."* Thought to date from around 4000 BC, the original was constructed of hewn timbers and ran across the Levels from the Polden ridge to the Isle of Westhay.

Burtle
Map 6 ref I7

5 miles NW of Glastonbury off the B3151

A lane to the west of Westhay leads to the village of Burtle, home of the impressive **Tom Mogg Inn**. Large and superbly equipped, this

Tom Mogg Inn

is a place where everything is catered for, be it food, drink, accommodation, wedding receptions, conferences, private discos, dinner dances, live entertainment or skittle parties. Resident proprietors Tom and Christine Presley are friendly and efficient hosts whose task it is to keep all the plates spinning.

Their seventeen guest bedrooms all have en suite facilities, and further accommodation is available in holiday bungalows for short or long lets. The large bar has an attractive dining area, and the separate restaurant offers a full ˆ la carte menu and has seating for a hundred diners. Very popular and excellent value, a carvery of roast beef, pork and turkey is available every Saturday evening and Sunday lunchtime until 4pm. *Tom Mogg Inn, Station Road, Burtle, Near Bridgwater, Somerset   Tel: 01278 722399*

Street   Map 6 ref J8
1 mile SW of Glastonbury on the A39

Historic Glastonbury has long been a conservation area whose growth has been severely restricted. No such restrictions, however, have applied to Street, a sprawling town lying a couple of miles to the southwest of Glastonbury whose population now approaches 10,000. A surprisingly ancient settlement which takes its name from the Roman road which ran close by, the oldest part is centred around the part 14th-century parish **Church of the Holy Trinity**. Most of the town, however, dates from the 19th century when it began to grow from a small rural village to the modern light industrial centre which can be seen today. The dramatic expansion was largely due to one entrepreneurial Quaker family, the Clarks. In the 1820s, Cyrus and James Clark began producing sheepskin slippers from the hides of local animals, and over the following century-and-a-half, their firm grew into one the largest manufacturers of quality shoes in Europe.

Many of the older buildings in Street owe their existence to the family, including the **Friends' Meeting House** of 1850, the clock tower, and the building which housed the original Millfield School. (The main part of the school has been relocated to the outskirts of the town.) The oldest part of the Clark's factory has now been converted into a fascinating footwear museum containing displays of historic shoes, shoe-making machinery, fashion photographs and exhibits chronicling the history of shoe design from Roman times to the present day. The company's headquarters are still located in Street, along with one of the first purpose-built factory shopping centres in Britain, the **Clark's Village**, one of several retail outlets in the town which claim to offer goods at factory prices.

Rumour Cafe-Bar and Restaurant

Following current trends and demands for an alternative to pubs. a new business to call in on is **Rumour Cafe-Bar and Restaurant**. A sister branch to Rumour in Totnes it is located just yards from the famous Clarkes Village. Hidden Places is now featuring quite a number of this type of continental style bar throughout the country and thier popularity is continually growing. A wide choice of food is available and is prepared to order. Daily changing specials as well as regular pizzas - made totally on the premises using traditional Mediterranean recipes - sandwiches, light meals and desserts are at most acceptable prices. The wine list has a great choice at sensible prices as too is the range of alcoholic drinks available at the bar. Children are catered for with meal portions and prices adjusted accordingly. The inside is airy and comfortable with a south facing garden offering level access to the upper floor for disabled clientele. *Rumour Restaurant, 62 Hish street, Street, Somerset BA16 0EQ Tel: 01458 447570*

Butleigh Wootton   *Map 6 ref J8*
2 miles S of Glastonbury off the B3151
The conspicuous columnar monument which can be seen on the ridge above Butleigh Wootton, a couple of miles to the southeast of Street,

is dedicated to Vice Admiral Sir Samuel Hood, a member of the celebrated family of naval officers who won a string of important maritime victories during the second half of the 18th century. **Butleigh Court** in Butleigh is an impressive Victorian pile built in 1845 which was damaged by fire and later divided into separate residential units.

Baltonsborough
Map6 ref K8

3 miles SE of Glastonbury off the A361

Baltonsborough, in the lanes two miles to the east, is the birthplace of St Dunstan, one of the greatest figures in the Anglo-Saxon church who rose to become abbot of Glastonbury Abbey and then Archbishop of Canterbury. A fine example of a medieval church house adjoins the parish churchyard; a rarity in Somerset, it once served the community as a brewery and village hall.

Shapwick
Map 6 ref I8

4 miles W of Glastonbury off the A39

The A39 to the west of Street runs along the crest of the Polden Hills, a long low ridge which, despite rising to less than 300ft, seems to dominate the surrounding countryside. Like everything else in this strange heathland landscape, the roads here are built on peat, giving them a curious spongy feel. The terrain around the village of Shapwick is scarred by an extensive peat-digging operation which over the years has extracted great quantities of this natural soil conditioner for use in suburban gardens. Nearby **Shapwick Heath Nature Reserve** provides a safe haven for rare plants and wildlife, although to enter, it is necessary to obtain a permit from the Nature Conservancy Council in Taunton. No such restrictions apply to the public footpath which sets out across undamaged moor to the northwest of the village.

Moorlinch
Map 6 ref I8

5 miles W of Glastonbury off the A39

The remote community of Moorlinch lies on the southern side of the A39, two miles to the southwest of Shapwick. This is the location of the **Moorlynch Vineyard**, an attractively situated 16-acre vineyard which offers wine tastings and tours of the winery. (Open daily except non-Bank Holiday Mondays, 10.30am to 5pm between May and September; also during Easter week.)

Bawdrip
Map 6 ref H8

4 miles NE of Bridgewater off the A39

The impressive **Knowle Inn** stands on the main A39 Glastonbury to

Knowle Inn

Bridgwater road at Bawdrip, three miles to the west of Chilton Polden and just two miles from junction 23 on the M5. Since taking over in 1996, Carol and Malcolm Singleton have tastefully upgraded the inn whilst taking care to retain its warm traditional character. They have also established a reputation for providing a warm welcome and some of the finest food and drink in the district. Along with a full selection of Whitbread ales, they offer an extensive range of home-cooked meals, including a special menu for children. The Knowle Inn has a skittle alley and a beer garden, and for those wishing to stay, there are also three comfortably-furnished letting rooms available throughout the year.*Knowle Inn, 115 Bath Road, Bawdrip, Near Bridgwater, Somerset Tel: 01278 683330 Fax: 01278 685646*

Westonzoyland   *Map 6 ref I8*
3 miles E of Bridgewater on the A372
The site of the last battle to be fought on English soil lies on the southern bank of what is now the **King's Sedgemoor Drain**, three miles to the south of Bawdrip. In July 1685, a field to the north of the village of Westonzoyland was the location of the Battle of Sedgemoor, a bloody encounter in which the well-equipped forces of King James II defeated the followers of the Duke of Monmouth to bring to an end the ill-fated *"Pitchfork Rebellion"*. Around 700 of Monmouth's

followers were slaughtered on the battlefield, and several hundred more were rounded up and taken to the churchyard at Westonzoyland where many were hanged. The Duke himself was taken to London where, ten days after the battle, he was executed on Tower Hill. However, it was during the infamous Judge Jeffreys' *"Bloody Assizes"* that the greatest terror was inflicted: well over 1000 men were condemned to death and summarily executed, and another 600 transported to the colonies. Today, the lonely battlefield is marked by a stark memorial.

Westonzoyland is also the site of an interesting steam-powered **Pumping Station** which was built in Victorian times to pump water into the River Parrett. The oldest of its kind in the Somerset Levels, the current engine, which replaced an earlier version dating from the 1830s, was in operation from 1861 to 1952. It has now been fully restored, entirely by volunteer labour, and is now Grade II star listed. The main engine can be seen in steam on New Year's Day, Bank Holiday Sundays and Mondays, and the first Sunday of the month between April and October. The site incorporates a small forge, a tramway and a number of exhibits from the age of steam, and is open Sundays and Bank Holiday Mondays, 2pm to 5pm, all year round; also Thursdays in June, July and August.

Burrow Bridge   *Map 6 ref I9*
4 miles SE of Bridgewater off the A361

Another interesting pumping station can be seen beside the River Parrett at Burrow Bridge, three miles to the south of Westonzoyland. It also contains a fine collection of Victorian pump engines and is open to the public on certain days each year. Burrow Bridge is also the location of the **Somerset Levels Basket and Craft Centre**, a workshop and showroom stocked with handmade basketware. (Open daily, 9am to 5.30pm, all year round.)

The conspicuous conical hill which can be seen nearby is known as **Burrow Mump**. This isolated knoll is reputed to be the site of an ancient fort belonging to King Alfred, the 9th-century King of Wessex, who is thought to have retreated to this lonely spot to escape a Viking incursion. It was during his time here that he is rumoured to have sought shelter in a hut in the nearby village of Athelney and was scolded by the family for burning their cakes. In many ways reminiscent of Glastonbury Tor, Burrow Mump is crowned by the picturesque remains of a medieval church which can be seen from miles around.

Burrow Mump is situated in the heart of the low-lying area known as the King's Sedge Moor, an attractive part of the Somerset Levels

Burrow Mump

which is drained by the rivers Cary (here renamed the King's Sedgemoor Drain) and Parrett. This rich area of wetland is known for its characteristic pollarded willows whose straight shoots, or withies, have been cultivated on a substantial scale ever since the taste for wicker developed during the Victorian era. The traditional craft of basket-making, one of Somerset's oldest commercial activities, once employed thousands of people. Though now very much scaled down, the industry is still alive and well and is even enjoying something of a revival.

Stoke St Gregory   *Map 6 ref I9*
6 miles SE of Bridgewater off the A361
Situated two and a half miles to the southwest of Burrow Mump, the village of Stoke St Gregory is the centre of Somerset's present-day wicker industry. Visitors to the ***Willows and Wetlands Centre*** can view the process of changing willow into finished baskets and wicker furniture. After the withies are cut, cleaned and boiled, they are woven into a wide variety of items using traditional methods which have been handed down for generations. Withies also provide the raw material for artist's charcoal. The centre contains a number of displays showing how the present Sedgemoor landscape has been created from marsh and swamp. It also has information on the many wild flowers, insects and birds which inhabit this unique wetland habitat.

Wells

The ancient ecclesiastical centre of Wells lies five miles along the A39 to the northeast of Glastonbury. With a population of under 10,000, this is the smallest city in England, and were it not for its cathedral and neighbouring bishop's palace, it would be unlikely to be more than an attractive small market town. However, the magnificent **Cathedral of St Andrew**, the first entirely Gothic structure of its kind in Britain, and its adjacent cathedral close undoubtedly make this one of the gems of north Somerset.

Deriving its name from a line of springs which rises from the base of the Mendips, King Ine of the West Saxons is believed to have founded the first church at Wells around 700 AD. After a diocesan tussle with Bath, the present cathedral was begun in the 12th century and took over three centuries to complete. As a consequence, it demonstrates the three main styles of Gothic architecture - Early English, Decorated and Perpendicular. Its 13th-century west front is generally considered to be its crowning glory: although defaced during the English Civil War, it incorporates over 100 larger-than-life-size statues of saints, angels and prophets who gaze down silently onto the cathedral lawn. The building's twin west towers were added a couple of centuries later; curious squat structures, they look as if they would benefit from the addition of spires.

The cathedral's many superb internal features include the beautiful and ingenious scissor arches which support the central tower, the great 14th-century stained-glass window over the high altar, the sweeping chapter house staircase with its elegant branching steps, and the great 14th-century astronomical clock, one of the oldest working timepieces in the world. This shows the minutes, hours and phases of the moon on separate inner and outer dials, and marks the quarter hours with a lively mechanised knights' tournament.

The 52-acre cathedral close is a tranquil city within a city. Indeed for many centuries, Wells functioned as two distinct entities: the ecclesiastical city and civic city. At that time, the parishioners were not welcomed into the cathedral and instead had to listen to the choir through strategically-placed holes in the cathedral walls. Similarly, the clergymen who died in the Black Death were buried under the cathedral green rather than in the town graveyard. The green itself is surrounded by a high wall which is breached at only three castellated entrance points. One of these sturdy gateways stands in the corner of the Market Place; known as **Penniless Porch**, it is where the bishop allowed the poor of the city to beg for alms from

Wells Cathedral

visitors entering the cathedral, a custom which appears to be back in fashion today.

The **Vicars' Close**, one of the oldest planned streets in Europe, lies on the northern side of the cathedral green. This remarkable cobbled thoroughfare was built in the mid 14th century, although the ornate chimneys were added a century later. Originally intended for cathedral choristers, it is still occupied by officers of the cathedral. The close is connected to the cathedral by a bridge which leads directly from the Vicars' Hall to the chapter house stairs. Known as the **Chain Gate**, it was built so that the innocent cathedral clergymen could avoid having to run the gauntlet of temptation by having to cross one of the town streets. (In a similar vein, the name of a thoroughfare in the town's former red light district was changed by the easily-affronted Victorians from Grope Lane to Union Street.)

The fortified **Bishop's Palace** is situated in an adjoining site to the south of the cathedral cloisters. This remarkable medieval building is surrounded by a moat which is fed by the springs which give the city its name. The palace is enclosed within a high stone wall, and in order to gain access from the Market Place, it is necessary to pass under a 13th-century arch known as the **Bishop's Eye** and then cross a drawbridge which was last raised for defensive purposes in 1831. Although still the official residence of the Bishop

Vicars' Close, Wells

of Bath and Wells, several parts are open to visitors, including the bishop's chapel and Jocelin's hall. (Open Tuesdays, Thursdays, Sundays and Bank Holiday Mondays, 11am to 6pm between 1 April and end-October.) The wide palace moat is home to a family of swans which are renowned for their ability to ask for food by ringing a bell on the wall below the gatehouse window. The impressive **Bishop's Tithe Barn** is situated to the south of the Bishop's Palace; in its day, it has served as a billet for Cromwell's troops and it is now used for private functions.

Other noteworthy buildings in Wells include the part 15th-century parish Church of St Cuthbert, which has such a lofty tower it is sometimes mistaken for the cathedral, and **Llewellyn's Almshouses** in Priest's Row. Founded 1614 and rebuilt between 1887 and 1901, these were originally constructed at the bequest of Henry Llewellyn who left £1600 to house *"ten elderly women."*

For those keen to find out more about the history of the locality, **Wells Museum**, near the west front of the cathedral, contains an interesting collection of locally-found artefacts. The splendid Cathedral Library possesses a number of rare books and manuscripts, a selection of which are on open display. The Market Place still hosts a lively street market on Wednesdays and Saturdays, or for those wanting a view of the city from a distance, an attractive footpath starts from Moat Walk and leads up onto the summit of Tor Hill.

Wells to Cheddar

Beryl   *Map 6 ref K7*
1 mile N of Wells off the A39

Beryl

Situated just a mile from the centre of Wells, ***Beryl*** is a small country mansion set in thirteen acres of beautiful grounds which offers truly exceptional bed and breakfast accommodation. Built in Gothic revival style as a hunting lodge in 1842, this superb house is filled with interesting architectural and decorative features of the period. The guest bedrooms all have fine country views and are luxuriously appointed with antique furniture, en suite facilities, direct-dial telephones and a full range of extras. Resident proprietor Holly Nowell offers outstanding hospitality and a delightful English breakfast, with dinner also being available by prior arrangement. *Beryl, Hawkers Lane, Wells, Somerset Tel: 01749 678738 Fax: 01749 670508*

Wedmore
Map 6 ref J6

6 miles W of Wells on the B3139

A pleasant drive to the west of Wells follows the old turnpike road across the low moors, now the B3139, to Wedmore, the ancient capital of the Somerset marshes. In 878 AD, King Alfred brought the newly-baptised Danish King Guthrum to this remote village to sign the Peace of Wedmore, a treaty which left Wessex in Alfred's hands and ceded East Anglia, East Mercia and the Kingdom of York to the Danes. Wedmore's largely-Perpendicular parish church of St Mary has a spectacular Norman south doorway which is thought to have been carved by the craftsmen who built Wells cathedral. The main street, the Borough, is lined with fine stone buildings, including the George, a lovely old coaching inn, and Church Street is a delightful thoroughfare with a grassy bank on one side which curves upward towards the church.

Westbury-sub-Mendip
Map 6 ref J6

3 miles NW of Wells on the A371

To the northwest of Wells, the A371 Cheddar road runs along the base of the Mendip escarpment, through an area which is renowned for its strawberries and soft fruit. Here, the landscape is scattered with attractive Mendip stone villages, including Westbury-sub-Mendip, one of the oldest settlements in Britain.

The Westbury Inn

Situated on the main road in the heart of Westbury-sub-Mendip, the **Westbury Inn** has a very welcoming appearance with plenty of hanging baskets, shrubs and tubs bursting with the colours of the season. In a recent nationwide competition, this impressive country inn and restaurant was voted the best in its class by Bass Brewery. Inside, the wonderful traditional atmosphere of an English country pub is enhanced by a fascinating collection of historic pictures of local life. Licensee Catherine Chauvet is a host with many years catering experience who takes great pride in providing real homemade food from the finest fresh ingredients. She offers a wide choice of both traditional and continental dishes, with a selection of daily specials and a special roast on Sundays. She also provides an excellent range of real ales and other quality drinks. Outside, there is a pleasant beer garden which has the added benefit of a secure children's play area. *Westbury Inn, Westbury-sub-Mendip, Near Wells, Somerset Tel: 01749 870223*

Wendy and Tony Thompson specialise in providing comfortable and relaxing holiday accommodation at **Stoneleigh House**, a tastefully-restored 18th-century farmhouse which is situated on the northern edge of the village. Their home has delightfully friendly and homely atmosphere, with flagstone floors, old beams and pine panelling.

Stoneleigh House

It also enjoys wonderful views over farmland and open countryside to distant Glastonbury Tor. The guest bedrooms are individually furnished, and some are equipped with en suite facilities. The generous farmhouse breakfast includes free range eggs and homemade preserves, with special options for vegetarians. Guests are invited to wander in the typically English country garden and enjoy its many interesting plants and wild flowers. (Unsuitable for smokers.) *Stoneleigh House, Westbury-sub-Mendip, Near Wells, Somerset Tel: 01749 870668*

Draycott
Map 6 ref J6

5 miles NW of Wells on the A371

Two miles to the northwest at Draycott, the **Strawberry Special** is a lovely old country pub which looks more like a smart Victorian detached home, with old stone walls surrounding the front terrace and colourful plants and flowers cascading from window boxes and hanging baskets. Well supported by locals, it is very pleasantly presented and serves good bar food and a wholesome and modestly-priced Sunday lunch.

Strawberry Special

The pub's name is derived from the trains which once took strawberries grown in the surrounding area to wholesalers across the UK. Before the line fell victim to the Beeching axe in 1963, fruit was loaded onto trains bound for Bristol and London at the old railway station opposite the pub. Those seeking an honest traditional English pub should make a point of calling in at the Strawberry Special. *Strawberry Special, Station Road, Draycott, Near Cheddar, Somerset Tel: 01934 742177*

Wookey Hole   *Map 6 ref K6*
1 mile NW of Wells off the A371

The minor roads to the northeast of the A371 Wells to Cheddar road ascend into the Mendip Hills, an area of rolling limestone upland which is popular with walkers, cavers and motorised sightseers. *Wookey Hole*, one of the best known visitor attractions in this Area of Outstanding Natural Beauty, lies on its southeastern edge, two miles to the northwest of Wells. Throughout the centuries, the carboniferous limestone core of the hills has been gradually dissolved by the small amount of carbonic acid in rainwater, an effect which has turned cracks into fissures, fissures into underground rivers and, on rare occasions, underground rivers into immense subterranean caverns such as these.

During the Palaeolithic and subsequent eras, Wookey Hole was lived in by wild animals such as lions, bears and woolly mammoths. Evidence of their occupation is supported by the large cache of prehistoric mammals' bones which was discovered in a recess known as the *Hyena's Den*, many of them showing the animals' teeth marks. There is also evidence of human occupation during the Iron Age. In total, there are over 25 caverns, although only the largest half dozen are open to visitors. The *Great Cave* contains a rock formation known as the Witch of Wookey which casts a ghostly shadow and is associated with gruesome legends of child-eating.

The river emerging from Wookey Hole, the Axe, has been harnessed to provide power for industrial use since the 16th century. Originally constructed in the mid-1800s as a paper mill, the present building on the site was acquired in 1973 by *Madame Tussaud's* who have installed a number of popular visitor attractions. These include an exhibition on the history of waxworks, a museum of Victorian fairground equipment, and a workshop where paper continues to be produced by hand. (Open daily, 9.30am to 5.30pm, all year round except December.)

Ebbor Gorge   *Map 6 ref K6*
2 miles NW of Wells off the A371

The National Trust-owned Ebbor Gorge lies about a mile to the northwest of Wookey Hole. A national nature reserve managed by English Nature, this dramatic landscape offers two scenic walks, the shorter of which takes around thirty minutes to complete and is suitable for wheelchair users accompanied by a strong pusher. The longer walks takes around an hour and a half and involves a certain amount of rock scrambling. The route climbs through woodland inhabited by badger and sparrowhawk, and passes close to caves which are home to greater and lesser horseshoe bats. From the top, buzzards can often be seen wheeling on the thermals above the gorge.

Priddy
Map 6 ref K6

3 miles NW of Wells off the B3135

Lying to the north of the Ebbor Gorge, the isolated settlement of Priddy is the highest village in Somerset. Once more important than it is today, its sizable part 13th-century church contains some interesting architectural oddities. The curious thatched structure on the green is a carefully-stacked pile of wooden hurdles. At one time, these were used to construct makeshift pens for Priddy's annual sheep fair, a colourful event which still takes place on the Wednesday closest to August 21. An impressive prehistoric site lies within a mile of the village to the northeast. Thought to be Bronze Age or earlier, *Priddy Circles* are composed of a series of raised banks surrounded by ditches. The nearby tumuli are known as the *Priddy Nine Barrows.*

Miners Arms

Priddy is also the location of one of the most impressive restaurants in the Mendips. Formerly a public house, the *Miners Arms* is now a delightful eating place which also provides comfortable overnight accommodation. Proprietors Pat and Bob Reynolds offer an imaginative choice of dishes, all freshly-prepared and beautifully-presented. On the evening we visited, main courses included Roquefort beef, vegetarian leek flan with red pepper sauce, and a local speciality, Priddy Oggy with cider sauce. There are also three modern and well-equipped letting rooms available for those wishing to stay. *Miners Arms, Priddy, Near Wells, Somerset   Tel: 01749 870217*

Mendip Heights Camping and Caravan Park

Mendip Heights, one of the loveliest camping and caravan parks in the area, is located on the western edge of Priddy, within easy reach of the Cheddar Gorge, Wells and Ebbor Gorge. Ideal for those who are looking for a peaceful and well-equipped place to stay, its many facilities include 90 pitches, 21 of which have electric hookups, a well-stocked shop and a heated toilet block with hot showers and laundry facilities. There is also a children's play area and a well-appointed six-berth mobile home available for hire. During the season, proprietors David and Ann Barnes organise a lively programme of outdoor activities, including caving, canoeing, mountain biking and archery. *Mendip Heights Camping and Caravan Park, Townsend, Priddy, Near Wells, Somerset   Tel/Fax: 01749 870241*

Cheddar   *Map 2 ref J6*
9 miles NW of Wells on the A371

A spectacular ravine, the **Cheddar Gorge**, carries the B3371 southwestwards towards the Somerset Levels. One of the most famous and often-visited natural attractions in Britain, it is characterised by towering cliffs of weathered limestone and precariously-rooted bands of undergrowth.

As well as being known for its gorge, the sprawling village of Cheddar is internationally-renowned for its caves and, of course, its cheese. Although much embellished by modern tourist paraphernalia, its two main show caverns, **Gough's Cave** and ***Cox's Cave***, are worth seeing for their sheer scale and spectacular calcite formations. (Both open daily, 10am to 5.30pm, all year round.) An almost complete skeleton dubbed *"Cheddar Man"* was discovered in Gough's Cave in 1903. This can now be seen in a nearby museum along with further evidence of human occupation of the caves, including flint and bone tools dating from the last Ice Age and artefacts from the Iron Age and the Romano-British period.

Starting from a little lower down the hill, the 322 steps of ***Jacob's Ladder*** lead up the side of the gorge to the site of ***Pavey's Lookout Tower***, a novel vantage point which offers a spectacular view of the surrounding landscape. An unusual market cross stands at the centre of the old part of Cheddar village. Really two crosses in one, a hexagonal superstructure was added to the original 15th-century preaching cross around a century later.

The Bath Arms Hotel in Bath Street is a lively establishment which is well supported by visitors and local customers alike. Run since 1986 by Jim Low, this pleasant hotel, bar and eating place is renowned for its warm and friendly atmosphere. The cosy and comfortable lounge bar is popular at lunchtimes for its excellent home-cooked food, and the Captain's Table restaurant has a pleasant nautical theme exemplified by a large ship's wheel mounted on the ceiling.

The Bath Arms Hotel

The restaurant is open from 8am for breakfast and morning coffee, and also provides lunches and evening meals with special diets being catered for by request. The larger King's Suite seats up to 100 people and is serviced directly from a newly-equipped kitchen. In 1941, the room was honoured by a visit from HM George VI, who enjoyed lunch here before going on to visit his troops at nearby Draycott. The Bath Hotel has nine guest bedrooms, all of which are equipped with TV, hospitality tray and telephone; most also have en suite facilities. The hotel has recently installed a fully-equipped children's playground and also has a wine shop to the rear which offers an interesting selection of wines and beers, some of which are unavailable on the supermarket shelves. *Bath Arms Hotel, Bath Street, Cheddar, Somerset Tel: 01934 742425*

The term Cheddar cheese refers to a recipe which was developed in the mid 19th century by Joseph Harding, a farmer and pioneer food scientist from near Bath who made the first scientific investigation into cheese-making. As the name refers to a recipe and not the place, the cheese can be made anywhere in the world; however, North Somerset is dotted with cheese manufacturers of various sizes, from single farmhouses to large-scale dairies. A number of these supplement their income by offering guided tours, craft demonstrations and catering facilities.

One of the prime visitor attractions in Somerset is the **Rural Village** of the Cheddar Gorge Cheese Company, the only firm in the world still making genuine Cheddar-made Cheddar cheese. Nestling at the foot of Cheddar Gorge, this unique 1920s-style village is a delightful reminder of the gentler pace of life of old Somerset and is the perfect setting for an enjoyable family day out. Visitors can experience some of the sights, sounds and tastes that previous generations knew. Attractions include a candle works, lace maker, fudge kitchen and the **Legbender Cider Barn** where adult visitors can sample real Somerset cider. There is also a cooperage where barrels are made by hand, a studio where wool is spun on a traditional spinning wheel, and a pottery where visitors can try their hand at the potters wheel.

No visit to the **Cheddar Gorge Cheese Company** would be complete without a tour of the cheese factory. Here, visitors can follow the fascinating process of traditional cheese-making from rich unpasturised local milk to rinded muslin-wrapped 56lb truckles. The cheese-makers give regular explanations and are always delighted to answer questions. Visitors are welcome to return to the factory as often as they like between visits to the other attractions on

Cheddar Gorge

Cheddar Gorge Cheese Co

the site. The Rural Village is located on the B3135 and is open every day from 10am between mid March and the end of October. *Cheddar Gorge Cheese Co, The Cliffs, Cheddar, Somerset Tel: 01934 742810*

Based at Cheddar in the heart of the beautiful North Somerset countryside, *Country Wide Weekends* offer enjoyable activity breaks which are designed for the fit and healthy, and those who would like to be. Here, everyone can participate as a resident or daily visitor in a wide range of outdoor activities, including caving, canoeing, climbing, abseiling, archery, guided night walks, and even off-road driving, all with first-class instruction.

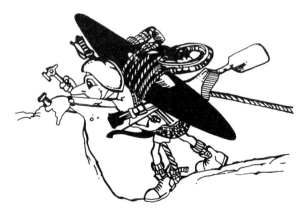

Country Wide Weekends

Age is no barrier, with all levels being catered for from seven years upwards. Participants are given the opportunity to take part in a variety of pursuits, and are invited to stretch their imagination with a programme designed to suit their individual abilities and budget. The organisers pay great attention to safety whilst ensuring the maximum enjoyment is derived from all activities so that everyone may benefit from this unique professional service. Great fun and great for the health, full details are available on request. *Country Wide Weekends, Activity Lodge, Broadway House, Cheddar, Somerset Tel: 01934 743775 Fax: 01934 744878*

Cheddar to Burnham-on-Sea

Charterhouse   Map 2 ref J5
3 miles NE of Cheddar off the B3371
Rising in places to over 1000ft above sea level, the Mendips form a landscape unlike any other in Somerset. Although it is hard to imagine today, these picturesque uplands were once an important lead and silver mining district, with the last mine at Priddy remaining open until 1908. Mendip lead-mining activity was centred around Charterhouse, a remote village lying four miles to the northwest of Priddy. The settlement takes its name from a Carthusian monastery, **Witham Priory**, which owned one of the four Mendip mining sectors, or Liberties. The area had been known for its mineral deposits since the Iron Age; indeed, such was its importance that the Romans declared its mines state property within six years of their arrival in Britain. Under Roman influence, silver and lead ingots, or pigs, were exported to France and Rome, and the settlement grew into a sizable town with its own fort and amphitheatre, the remains of which can be still be out today. Improved technology in later centuries allowed for the reworking of the original seams, and the area is now littered with abandoned mine buildings and smelting houses.

Burrington Combe   Map 2 ref J5
3 miles N of Cheddar on the B3134
A path from Charterhouse church leads up onto the 1067ft **Black Down**, the highest point in the Mendips. To the northwest, the B3134 descends through Burrington Combe, a deep cleft which is said to have provided the Reverend Augustus Toplady with the inspiration for his hymn, Rock Of Ages.

Axbridge
Map 2 ref I6

1 mile W of Cheddar off the A371

To the west of Cheddar, the A371 skirts around Cheddar's curious circular reservoir before passing to the north of Axbridge, an ancient small town with a delightful centre which is well worth making a detour to visit. During the Saxon era, Axbridge was a fortified market town which had its own mint, then in the late medieval period, it was a prosperous wool centre which made its living processing Mendip fleeces into woven cloth. Although nothing whatsoever to do with the monarch in question, **King John's Hunting Lodge** in the Square is an exceptional example of a half-timbered merchant's house dating from around 1500. (Its name is a reminder that the Mendip hills were once a royal hunting forest.) Now owned by the National Trust, it was extensively restored in the 1970s and now houses an excellent local museum. (Open daily, 2pm to 5pm between Easter and end-September.)

The magnificent parish **Church of St John** also overlooks the Square. A fine example of Somerset Perpendicular, it stands at the top of an impressive flight of steps and contains some exceptional monumental brasses and stained glass. The centre of Axbridge contains an unusual number of handsome Georgian shops and town houses and is best explored on foot.

Lower Weare
Map 2 ref I6

2 miles W of Cheddar on the A38

Those with an interest in tropical birds should make a point of finding the **Ambleside Bird Gardens** at Lower Weare, a village situated two miles to the west of Axbridge near the point the A38 crosses the River Axe. (Open daily, 10am to 5pm between early-March and late-October.) A minor road to the northwest of here leads to the hamlet of Webbington Loxton, home of an interesting visitor attraction, the **Wheelwright's Working Museum** and **Gypsy Folklore Collection**. (Open Wednesdays to Sundays (daily in July, August and September), 10am to 6pm, all year round.)

Chapel Allerton
Map 2 ref I6

4 miles SW of Cheddar off the B3151

The only complete windmill in Somerset can be found in the lanes to the south of Lower Weare in the village of Chapel Allerton. Well worth making a detour to visit, this superb 18th-century stone-built **Tower Mill** still was once the principal flour mill for the locality. (Open Sundays and Bank Holiday Mondays, 2.30pm to 4.30pm between Easter and end-September; also Wednesdays in July and August; admission free.)

Brent Knoll   *Map 1 ref H6*
9 miles SW of Cheddar off the B3140

The A38 to the southwest of Lower Weare leads over the M5 motorway to Brent Knoll, a conspicuous landmark which can be seen from as far away as South Wales. Before the Somerset Levels were drained, this isolated hill would almost certainly have been an island. Like many other natural features of the landscape which appear out of place, there are stories that the knoll owes its existence to the Devil. It rises to 445ft and is topped by the remains of an Iron Age hill fort. Several centuries later, its southern slope is reputed to have been the site of a battle against the Danes which was fought and won by King Alfred. The summit, which can be reached by way of footpaths starting near the churches at East Brent and Brent Knoll, affords a spectacular view over the surrounding landscape.

The churches at East Brent and Brent Knoll are both exceptional. The former has a superb 17th-century plasterwork ceiling and a collection of carved bench ends which incorporate the abbot of Glastonbury's coat of arms and initials. The latter also contains an interesting series of bench ends which tell the cryptic story of how the local parishioners, who are represented by geese and other creatures, won a dispute with the 15th-century abbot, who is represented by a fox.

Berrow   *Map 1 ref H6*
10 miles SW of Cheddar on the B3140

The B3140 to the west of Brent Knoll leads to Berrow and Brean, two ancient settlements on the Bristol Channel coast which have been overwhelmed by 20th-century development. Each has a part 13th-century church which looks somewhat out of place amongst the surrounding seaside attractions.

One of the most absorbing visitor attractions in the area can be found in Red Road on the edge of Berrow. The *Animal Farm Country Park* is set in 25 acres of lovely Somerset countryside and is the perfect setting for a family day out. Whether visitors go to feed the animals, let off steam in the play areas, or enjoy some refreshments in the old barn tearoom, there is plenty for all ages to see and do. Animal Farm is the ideal classroom, providing many children with their first hands-on experience of animals in a rural environment.

Many new and exciting attractions are added each year, a feature which encourages visitors to return again and again to meet old

Animal Farm Country Park

friends and make new ones. A place for a highly enjoyable family day
out, Animal Farm is situated around 45 minutes drive from Bristol,
Bath and Taunton. (Telephone for further details.) *Animal Farm
Country Park, Red Road, Berrow, Nr. Burnham-on-Sea, Somerset
Tel: 012787 751628*

Brean Down   Map 1 ref H5
10 miles W of Cheddar off the A370
The magnificent sandy beach to the north of Berrow is over five miles
long. At its northern margin, it is sheltered by the 320ft high Brean
Down, an imposing remnant of the Mendip hills which projects into
the Bristol Channel. (Another fragment can be seen in the shape of
the offshore island, **Steep Holm**). The remains of an Iron Age coastal
fort and a Roman temple have been discovered on the Down which
is now a designated nature reserve under the protection of the
National Trust. The Victorian fortifications at the western tip were
partially demolished in 1900 when a soldier accidentally fired his
rifle into the ammunition store. With one of the widest tidal ranges
in Europe, the currents around the headland can be dramatic and
very dangerous.

Burnham-on-Sea   Map1 ref H6
10 miles SW of Cheddar on the B3140
Further south, Burnham-on-Sea is a sizable seaside town with a
wide sandy beach which at low tide seems to extend for miles. When
mineral springs were discovered here in the late 18th century, an
attempt was made to reinvent the resort as a spa town to rival

Cheltenham and Bath. However, the efficacious effects of its waters were never properly demonstrated and in the end it had to fall back on its beach to attract visitors. The west tower of the part 14th-century parish church has a worrying lean owing to its sandy foundations. Inside, there is a remarkable Jacobean altarpiece which was originally made for Whitehall Palace; designed by Sir Christopher Wren, the carving has been attributed to Grinling Gibbons. The Low Lighthouse, the curious square structure raised above the beach on tall stilts, is perhaps Burnham's most distinctive landmark.

Those looking for superior bedand breakfast accommodation within easy walking distanceof Burnham's town centre and beach should make a point of finding Prior's Mead in Rectory Road. A handsome Edwardian residence standing in a quiet road just two miles from junction 22 on the M5, it is set within its own beautiful grounds containing a swimming pool, croquet lawn and mature weeping willows.

Prior's Mead

The three guest rooms are comfortable and attractively furnished; one has the added benefit of en suite facilities, and two have their own private facilities. All bedrooms have king-sized beds, remote-control colour TV and tea and coffee making facilities. Proprietors Fizz and Peter Alexander provide superb hospitality and one of the best English breakfasts in the district. They also offer reduced terms for stays of three nights or more. *Prior's Mead, 23 Rectory Road, Burnham-on-Sea, Somerset TA8 2BZ Tel: 01278 782116 Mobile: 0860 573018*

Highbridge   *Map 1 ref H7*
10 miles SW of Cheddar on the A38

AdjoiningBurnham-on-Sea to the southeast, the small townof Highbridge was once a busy coastal port at the mouth of the Glastonbury Canal. A couple of noteworthy places of interest lie within easy driving distance of here. The **Badger and Wildlife Rescue Centre** at East Huntspill offers a wide range of attractions and activities related to the wildlife of the area, including a badger observation set, bee hives and nature trail. Situated off the B3141, it is open daily, 10am to 6pm, all year round.

Mark   *Map 1 ref I6*
6 miles SW of Cheddar on the B3139

A couple of miles further east in the village of Mark, **Coombes Somerset Cider** is located at Japonica Farm on the B3139 Wells road. Founded in 1919, this family-owned firm still makes cider in the traditional way, using local apple varieties and maturing the cider in oak vats. Visitors can see the process of cider making from start to finish and sample the end product. There is also a video presentation of cider maker's year, an interesting museum and a tearoom. (Open Mondays to Saturdays, 9am to 6pm, all year round; admission free.)

Blackford   *Map 1 ref I6*
5 miles SW of Cheddar on the B3139

The attractive village of Blackford lies on the northern side of the B3139 Wedmore road, a couple of miles to the east of Mark. This is the location of the **Sexeys Arms** Inn, a delightful pub and eating place which is run by John and Cheryl Edwards. (From junction 22 of the M5, follow the A38 towards Bristol, then take the first turning southeast towards the village of Mark; after approximately two miles, turn east onto the B3139, then travel through Mark and on to Blackford; the Sexeys Arms is on the left.) This quaint old inn is named after Hugh Sexey, a poor farmer's son born in Bruton in 1556 who went on to become one of the auditors to Elizabeth I who, in recognition of his services, bestowed the estate of Blackford to him. Today, John and Cheryl are gaining their own recognition with some very impressive food, drink and hospitality. The menu features an imaginative and moderately-priced selection that changes daily, and

The Sexeys Arms

with such tempting dishes as ribbed eye steak, monkfish Provencal and Dorset trout, diners are sure to enjoy their meal.*Sexeys Arms, Blackford, Nr. Wedmore, Somerset Tel: 01934 712487*

CHAPTER FIVE
South Somerset

Perry's Cider Mills

5
South Somerset

Around Taunton

A good place to begin a tour of South Somerset is from the **Wellington Monument**, the conspicuous 170ft obelisk which stands on a spur of the Blackdown hills overlooking the Vale of Taunton Deane. This striking landmark was constructed in honour of the Duke of Wellington on the estate bought for him by the nation following his victory at the Battle of Waterloo. (Despite his adopted title, the Duke had no connections with the locality and is known to have visited the estate only once in thirty years.)

The monument's foundation stone was laid in 1817 following a wave of enthusiastic public support. However, the necessary funds to complete the project did not materialise and a number of radical economies had to be introduced. These included the redesigning of the structure to give it three sides instead of four and the cancelling of an ostentatious cast iron statue of the Duke which had been proposed for the top. As it was, the modified triangular pinnacle remained unfinished until 1854, two years after Wellington's death. Visitors can still make the formidable 235-step climb to the top where they are rewarded with spectacular views across lowland Somerset to Exmoor and the Mendips.

Travelling eastwards, the B3170 to the south of Taunton skirts Taunton Racecourse, then a little further on, a lane to the west leads to **Poundisford Park**, a small H-shaped Tudor mansion standing within a delightful wooded deer park which once belonged to the bishops of Winchester. The house is renowned for its fine plasterwork ceilings and the grounds incorporate a formal garden laid out in the Tudor style. (Open Wednesdays and Thursdays, 11am to 5pm between early-May and mid-September; also Fridays in July and August.)

North Curry
Map 5 ref H9
4 miles E of Taunton off the A378

The **Bird in Hand** is a delightful country inn which lies in the lanes to the north of the A378 Langport road, five miles to the east of Taunton. Situated in the lovely old village of North Curry, it can be easily reached from junction 25 on the M5 by taking the A358 Ilminster road and then turning east at Thornfalcon traffic lights. Well worth making the effort to find, this attractive family-run free house has a red pantiled roof and striking white-painted walls adorned with climbing shrubs and hanging baskets of flowers. The interior has an equally inviting character, with flag-stoned floors, beamed ceilings and a wonderful traditional atmosphere.

Bird in Hand

Resident proprietors Dianne and Jeremy Hook provide a warm welcome and some of the finest food and drink in the area. Along with a range of traditional ales, they serve an imaginative choice of home-cooked fare, including vegetarian, continental and English dishes, either served in the bar or the intimate atmosphere of the candlelit restaurant. They also offer a special menu for younger diners. A popular roast carvery is available at lunchtime on Sundays for which advance booking is advised. The Bird in Hand also has a sunny terrace to the front, a safe garden to the rear, and an unusual self-contained skittle alley. *Bird in Hand, North Curry, Near Taunton, Somerset Tel: 01823 490248*

Hatch Beauchamp
Map 2 ref H10
5 miles SE of Taunton off the A358

One of the finest country houses in the area can be found at Hatch

Beauchamp, just off the A358 Ilminster road, five miles to the southeast of Taunton. Built of attractive honey-coloured limestone in two phases during the second half of the 18th century, **Hatch Court** was designed in impressive Palladian style by the Axbridge architect, Thomas Prowse. Among its finest features are the hall with its cantilevered stone staircase, the curved orangery with its arched floor-to-ceiling windows, and the semicircular china room with its elegant display of rare porcelain and glass. There is also a fine collection of 17th and 18th-century English and French furniture, 19th and 20th-century paintings, and a small military museum commemorating Britain's last privately-raised regiment, the Princess Patricia's Canadian Light Infantry. The extensively restored grounds incorporate a walled kitchen garden, rose garden, arboretum and deer park. (Open Thursdays and Bank Holiday Mondays, 2.30pm to 5.30pm between mid-June and mid-September.)

Ilminster to Yeovil

Ilminster   *Map 6 ref I11*
9 mile SE of Taunton on the B3168

The old ecclesiastical and agricultural centre of Ilminster lies near the junction of the A358 and A303, five miles southeast of Hatch Beauchamp. Meaning *"minster on the River Isle"*, the settlement takes its name from church which was founded here by the Saxon King Ine in the 8th century. The borough was recorded in the Domesday Book as having a market and three mills, and during the medieval era it grew to become a thriving wool and lace-making town. This period of prosperity is reflected in the town's unusually large parish church, a magnificent 15th-century minster whose massive multi-pinnacled tower is modelled on Wells cathedral. Thanks to a Georgian restoration the interior is surprisingly plain; however, it does contain a number of interesting tombs and monumental brasses. A stroll around the old part of Ilminster reveals a number of lovely old buildings, many of which are constructed of golden Ham stone. These include the chantry house, the old grammar school and the colonnaded market house.

Dillington House, on the northern outskirts of Ilminster, is a handsome part-Tudor mansion which is the former home of the Speke family. In the time of James II, John Speke was an officer in the Duke of Monmouth's ill-fated rebel army which landed at Lyme Regis in 1685. However, following its disastrous defeat at Sedgemoor, he was forced to flee abroad, leaving his brother, George, who had done no more than shake the Duke's hand, to face the wrath of Judge

Jeffreys. The infamous Hanging Judge sentenced poor George to death, justifying his decision with the words, *"His family owes a life and he shall die for his brother."* Dillington House is currently leased to Somerset County Council and functions as an adult education centre.

Three miles to the northeast of Ilminster, a lane to the east of the B3168 leads the beautiful National Trust-owned *Barrington Court*. The house was built in the 1570s from local Ham stone and displays the characteristics of the architectural transformation from Tudor Gothic, with its buttresses and mullioned and transomed windows, to Renaissance, with its twisted finials and chimney stacks. The garden was laid out in the 1920s in a series of themed rooms, including the iris garden, lily garden, white garden and fragrant rose garden. The celebrated landscape architect, Gertrude Jekyll, was brought in to advise on the initial planting and layout, and the garden remains the finest example of her work in the Trust's care. There is also an exceptionally attractive one-acre kitchen garden with apple, pear and plum trees trained along the walls which in season produces fruit and vegetables for use in the restaurant. (House and garden open daily, except Fridays, 11am to 5.30pm between late-March and end-October.) The nearby estate village of Barrington contains some fine old Ham-stone cottages.

Shepton Beauchamp   *Map 6 ref I10*
3 miles NE of Ilminster off the A303
The remains of a medieval open strip field system can still be made out at Shepton Beauchamp, a mile to the southeast of Barrington Court, or for some heritage of a different kind it is worth visiting Westport, on the B3168 one and a half miles to the north. This tranquil community is a former inland port which was built at the height of the canal era by the Parrett Navigation Company for exporting wool and stone and importing coal and building materials.

Dowlish Wake   *Map 6 ref I11*
1 mile S of Ilminster off the B3168
Those with an interest in traditional cider making should make a point of finding *Perry's Cider Mills* at Dowlish Wake, a pleasant community which lies hidden in the lanes to the southeast of Ilminster.

The village contains some attractive honey-coloured Ham-stone cottages and an imposing parish church which stands on a steep rise a little way from the centre. Inside can be seen the tomb of John Hanning Speke, an intrepid Victorian explorer who journeyed for

Perry's Cider Mills, Dowlish Wake

over 2500 miles through some of the harshest terrain in Africa to confirm Lake Victoria as the source of the River Nile. Speke returned to England a hero, but tragically, on the very morning he was due to report his findings to the British Geographical Association, he accidentally shot himself while out partridge shooting.

Chard
Map 6 ref H12

4 miles SW of Ilminster on the A358

On the northern approaches to Chard, the A358 Ilminster to Axminster road passes close to two contrasting places of interest. To the west, **Hornsbury Mill** is a 200-year-old corn mill which has an impressive working water wheel, and to the east, **Chard Reservoir Nature Reserve** is a conservation area which offers a varied two-mile circular walk through rustling reed beds, broad-leaved woodland and open hay meadows. An important habitat for wildlife, the lake is home to a number of rare bird species, including the kingfisher and great crested grebe.

Chard, in the southwest corner of Somerset, is a pleasant light industrial town whose population of 12,000 has more than doubled since the Second World War. The borough has Saxon origins, and during medieval times it was a prosperous wool centre with its own mayor, or portreeve, and burgesses. However, with the exception of the fine Perpendicular parish church, few buildings date from before 1577, the year of the devastating fire which razed most of the town to the ground. (Perhaps this is how Chard got its name?)

Chard's gradual reconstruction has left it with some fine 17th-century buildings, including the courthouse and old grammar school,

Chard & District Museum, Chard

and there are also a number of striking Georgian and Victorian structures, most notably the neoclassical town hall of 1835 with its impressive two-tier portico. An unusual round toll house with a conical thatched roof can also be seen on the outskirts of the town.

Despite its rapid postwar development, the centre retains a pleasant village-like atmosphere which is particularly apparent around the broad sloping main street. A good way to find out more about the town's eventful past is to visit the award-winning **Chard Museum** in Godworthy House. This impressive local museum is housed in an attractive thatched building at the west end of the High Street and is open on Mondays to Saturdays (plus Sundays in July and August), 10.30am to 4.30pm between early-May and mid-October.

Wambrook   *Map 6 ref H12*
6 miles SW of Ilminster off the A30
Those with an interest in animal welfare should make a point of visiting the **Ferne Animal Sanctuary** at Wambrook. Situated off the A30 a couple of miles to the west of Chard, this delightful establishment was originally founded in 1939 by the Duchess of Hamilton and Brandon when she lived at Berwick St John near Shaftesbury. Since 1975, it has been located in its present position overlooking the valley of the River Yarty on a 51-acre site which incorporates a nature trail, conservation area, dragonfly pools and picnic areas. Its purpose is to accept any animal whose life is in danger for which there is suitable accommodation. Around 300

animals are cared for at any one time, including horses, donkeys, pigs, goats, dogs, cats, ducks and rabbits. In addition, caring homes are actively sought for cats and dogs.

Ferne Animal Sanctuary

The Ferne Animal Sanctuary also has a well-stocked gift shop and a welcoming tearoom which is open on Wednesdays, Saturdays, Sundays and Bank Holiday Mondays, 2pm to 5pm between 1 April and 30 September. Admission is free, and there are good facilities for disabled visitors. Various schemes are available for those who would like to help this very worthy cause, which is a Registered Charitable Trust No. 245671. Please contact the sanctuary for an informative booklet and further details about sponsorship or arranging a deed of covenant. For those with an interest in animals and their welfare, a visit to the Ferne Animal Sanctuary is a must. *Ferne Animal Sanctuary, Wambrook, Near Chard, Somerset Tel: 01460 65214*

Cricket St Thomas   *Map 6 ref I12*
4 miles S of Ilminster off the A30
The former estate village of Cricket St Thomas lies on the A30, three miles to the east of Chard. This once-secluded hamlet is now the home of one of Britain's least hidden places, Noel Edmonds' **Crinkley Bottom** television theme park (formerly the Cricket St Thomas Wildlife and Leisure Park). Although it may be hard to imagine today, Cricket House was once the family home of the great 18th-century naval commander, Admiral Sir Alexander Hood, and later of the Bristol chocolate manufacturer, F J Fry. Today, it is marketed

as the *"Grantleigh Manor"* of the BBC television comedy series, To The Manor Born. The estate incorporates the tiny church of St Thomas with its impressive monument to Admiral Hood, later Viscount Bridport. Other attractions include a horse stables, children's adventure fort, wildlife world, and a varied assortment of themed crowd pullers designed to bait the very young. (Open all hours.)

Forde Abbey, Nr Cricket St Thomas

One of the loveliest country houses in England lies in the lanes to the south of Cricket St Thomas. Set in the beautiful valley of the River Axe, **Forde Abbey** was founded as a Cistercian monastery in the 12th century and took over four centuries to complete. To prevent its destruction following the Dissolution of the Monasteries in 1539, the abbot offered the property to the crown and it became a private mansion. Today, it is the family home of the Ropers and contains an outstanding collection of tapestries, period furniture, and paintings.

The refectory, dormitory and chapter house survive from the medieval monastery which is surrounded by thirty acres of superbly landscaped grounds encompassing lakes, a bog garden, nursery and walled kitchen garden. The estate is also known for its pedigree herd of cattle and incorporates a pick-your-own fruit farm. (House open Sundays, Wednesdays and Bank Holidays, 1pm to 4.30pm between 1 April and 31 October; gardens open daily, all year round.)

Clapton
Map 6 ref I12

6 miles SE of Ilminster on the B3165

Another delightful landscaped garden can be found beside the B3165, four miles to the east of Forde Abbey. The ten-acre **Clapton Court Gardens** are some of the most varied and interesting in Somerset. Among the many beautiful features are the formal terraces, rose garden, rockery and water garden. The grounds incorporate a large wooded area containing a massive ash tree which, at over 230 years old and 28ft in girth, is believed to be the oldest and largest in mainland Britain. There is also a fine metasequoia which is already over 80ft tall, having been planted in 1950 from seed brought back from China. (Open Tuesdays to Thursdays, 2pm to 5pm between 1 April and 30 September.)

Mosterton
Map 6 ref J12

8 miles SE of Ilminster on the A3066

In the village of Mosterton, three miles further east on the A3066 Crewkerne to Bridport road, David, Benjamin and Simon Eeles produce a unique range of handmade stoneware and porcelain at the **Eeles Family Pottery**. At certain times, visitors can view the pots being thrown and decorated before they are taken for firing in the family's three-chambered dragon kiln.

Crewkerne
Map 6 ref J12

6 miles SE of Ilminster on the A356

The ancient former market town of Crewkerne lies at the junction of the A30 and A356, three miles to the north of Mosterton. Like Chard and Ilminster, the town developed as a thriving agricultural and market centre during Saxon times and even had its own mint in the decades leading up to the Norman invasion. The magnificent parish church of St Bartholomew was built on the wealth generated by the late-medieval boom in the wool industry. A structure of minster-like proportions, it is one of the grandest of the many fine Perpendicular churches to be found in south Somerset.

Unlike most other towns in Wessex whose textile industries suffered an almost total decline, Crewkerne was rejuvenated in the 18th century when the availability of locally-grown flax led to an expansion in the manufacture of sailcloth and canvas webbing. Among the many thousands of sails to be made here were those for HMS Victory, Nelson's flagship at the Battle of Trafalgar. The town's resurgence was further boosted by the development of the London-Exeter coaching route at this time, a factor which led to the rebuilding of old Crewkerne in elegant Georgian style. Many fine town houses and inns from this period can still be seen in the centre, most notably in Church and Abbey streets, now an Area of Outstanding Architectural Interest. Less appealing are the northern and southern outskirts of the town which been given up to large-scale light industrial development.

The A30 to the west of Crewkerne climbs onto the aptly-named **Windwhistle Hill**, a high chalk-topped ridge which enjoys dramatic views southwards to Lyme Bay and northwards across the Somerset Levels to the mountains of South Wales. This is also the location of the impressive Windwhistle golf and country club.

Hinton St George   Map 6 ref I11
5 miles SE of Ilminster off the A356

A lane to the north of Windwhistle Hill leads to the former estate village of Hinton St George, an unspoilt Ham-stone gem which for centuries was owned, and left virtually untouched, by the Poulett family. The Pouletts rebuilt Hinton House shortly after their arrival here in the 15th century, and this structure now forms the core of the present-day mansion. This has now been converted into apartments, although local people say it continues to be haunted by the ghost of a young Poulett woman who died of a broken heart after her father shot dead the man she was planning to elope with.

Several ostentatious monuments to members of the Poulett family can be seen in the superb little 15th-century church of St George. With its pinnacled tower and imposing interior, this is perhaps the most outstanding feature of the village. Another noteworthy building is the so-called priory, a 16th-century residence with a 14th-century window at its eastern end which is thought to have once belonged to Monkton Farleigh Priory in Wiltshire. It is a tradition for Hinton children to beg candles to put inside their intricately-fashioned turnip and pumpkin lanterns on *"Punkie Night"*, the last Thursday in October. It is thought to be very unlucky to refuse them, as each lantern is said to represent the spirit of a dead person who, unless illuminated, will rise up at Hallowe'en.

Haselbury Plucknett   Map 6 ref J11
5 miles SW of Yeovil on the A3066

The A30 to the northeast of Crewkerne crosses the upper reaches of the River Parrett before being joined by the A3066 Bridport road. The delightfully-named community of Haselbury Plucknett lies half a mile south of this junction. Another gem of a village, it has a large part-Norman church whose churchyard contains a series of unusual *"squeeze stones"*.

West Coker   *Map 6 ref K11*
2 miles SW of Yeovil on the A30

Continuing northeastwards on the A30, the magnificent **Brympton d'Evercy Manor House** lies in the lanes to the north of West Coker, two and a half miles from the centre of Yeovil. Norman in origin but with major 16th and 17th-century additions, it has a superb golden Ham-stone south wing which was built in Jacobean times to a design influenced by Inigo Jones. It many fine internal features include the longest straight single-span staircase in Britain and an unusual modern tapestry showing an imaginary bird's eye view of the property in the 18th century. The little estate church of St Andrew boasts a sturdy square bell tower and some fine medieval monuments. When seen from a distance, the mansion, church and nearby dower house make a delightful lakeside grouping. (Open by appointment only by telephoning 01935 862528.)

Yeovil to Somerton

Yeovil   *Map 6 ref K11*
18 miles W of Taunton on the A30

With its 28,000 inhabitants and strategic position at the junction of several main routes, **Yeovil** is the largest centre of population in south Somerset. A modern light industrial and market town whose best-known employer is Westland Helicopters, it offers a comprehensive range of shopping and recreational facilities. Despite its up-to-date character, Yeovil's origins go back to the time of the ancient Romans. During the Middle Ages, a lively livestock and produce market was established in the town which continues to be held here every Friday.

Yeovil's parish **Church of St John the Baptist** is the only significant medieval structure to survive, most of its other early buildings having been destroyed in a series of town fires in the 17th century. A substantial Ham-stone structure dating from the second half of the 14th century, the church has surprisingly austere exterior given its exceptional number of windows. (Indeed, it has so many that it is sometimes referred to as the *"lantern of the West"*). Perhaps its finest internal feature is the plain brass lectern which is believed to date from around 1450. One of only five still in existence, it is the only one to be found in a parish church.

During the 18th century, Yeovil developed into a flourishing coaching and industrial centre whose output included gloves, leather, sailcloth and cheese. This rapid expansion was enhanced by the arrival of the railway in the mid 19th century, then in the 1890s, James Petter, a local ironmonger and pioneer of the internal combustion engine, founded a business which went on to become one of the largest manufacturers of diesel engines in Britain. Although production was eventually transferred to the Midlands, a subsidiary set up to produce aircraft during the First World War has since evolved into the present-day helicopter plant.

Corinthians House

Those looking for first-rate accommodation in a very pleasant and peaceful part of Yeovil should make a point of finding **Corinthians House**, a detached private residence which lies just five minutes' walk from the town centre. Proprietor Derek Ridler offers a warm welcome at this quiet and comfortable home-from-home. An experienced caterer and cook, he serves a delicious a la carte breakfast and can also provide delicious dinners by prior arrangement. Each of the guest bedrooms is well-furnished and equipped with a colour television and complimentary tray. Children are most welcome at Corinthians, which is conveniently located for exploring Yeovil and the many other places of interest which lie within easy driving distance. *Corinthians House, 15 Park Gardens, Yeovil, Somerset Tel: 01935 420909*

A fascinating museum documenting the social and industrial history of the area from prehistoric and Roman times through to the agricultural and industrial revolutions can be found near the Octagon Theatre in the centre of Yeovil. Situated in Wyndham House in Hendford, the recently-refurbished **Museum of South Somerset** uses a series of imaginative settings to recapture the atmosphere of the times. (Open Tuesdays to Saturdays, 10am to 4pm, all year round; closed Saturdays in winter; admission free.) The **Goldenstones Leisure Centre** in Ninesprings, Yeovil is an impressive leisure facility which incorporates a 25 metre pool, hi tech gym, sauna, solariums and bistro. (Open daily throughout the year.)

Barwick   *Map 6 ref K11*
2 miles S of Yeovil off the A37

Two miles south of Yeovil, a turning to the east off the A37 leads to Barwick Park (pronounced Barrik), an estate dotted with bizarre follies which were built in the 1830s by local landowner, George Messiter, to employ out-of-work glove-makers. Arranged at the four points of the compass, the eastern folly known as *"Jack the Treacle Eater"* is composed of a rickety stone arch topped by a curious turreted room. According to local lore, it is named after a foot messenger who ran back and forth to London on a diet of nothing but bread and treacle. The estate also possesses a curious grotto and a handsome church with a Norman font and an unusual 17th-century transeptal tower.

Compton   *Map 6 ref K10*
2 miles E of Yeovil off the A30

The world-renowned **Compton House** lies beside the A30 Sherborne road, a couple of miles across the Dorset border to the east of Yeovil. This is the location of the unique **Worldlife Conservation Centre**, formerly Worldwide Butterflies, and Lullingstone Silk Farm, Britain's only working silk farm. The beautiful grounds incorporate a Butterfly Jungle populated by spectacular free-flying butterflies and giant moths, a series of informative environmental displays, a 12th-century church, and an appealing collection of peacocks, doves and other unusual creatures. (Open daily, 10am to 5pm between early April and 30 September.)

Montacute   *Map 6 ref J10*
4 miles NW of Yeovil off the A3088

On the opposite side of Yeovil, the superb National Trust-owned

Montacute House lies on the southern side of the A3088 Martock road, four miles to the west of the town centre. The present mansion was built in the 1580s by Edward Phelips, Queen Elizabeth's Master of the Rolls, and is considered a masterpiece of Renaissance architecture. Constructed of golden Ham stone to an H-shaped design, it is adorned with characteristic open parapets, fluted columns, twisted pinnacles, oriel windows and carved statues. The long gallery, one the grandest of its kind in Britain, houses a fine collection of Tudor and Jacobean portraits which are on permanent loan from London's National Portrait Gallery. Other noteworthy features include the stone and stained-glass screen in the great hall, and Lord Curzon's bath, an Edwardian addition which is concealed in a bedroom cupboard. An established story tells of how Curzon, a senior Tory politician, waited at Montacute in 1923 for news that he was to be called to form a new government. The call never came.

Montacute House stands within a magnificent landscaped park which incorporates a walled formal garden, a fig walk, an orangery, and a cedar lawn formerly known as *"Pig's Wheaties's Orchard"*. (House open daily except Tuesdays, 12 noon to 5.30pm between late-March and end-October; grounds open all year round.)

500 years before the present Elizabethan house was built, a controversial castle was constructed on the nearby hill by William the Conqueror's half-brother, Robert, Count of Mortain. The Saxons were angered by his choice of site, for they believed it to be a holy place where King Alfred had buried a fragment of Christ's cross. In 1068, they rose up and attacked the castle in one of the many unsuccessful piecemeal revolts against the Norman occupation. Ironically, a subsequent Count of Mortain was found guilty of treason and forced into founding, and then donating all his lands to, a Cluniac priory on the site now occupied by Montacute village. The castle has long since disappeared, as has the monastery, with the exception of its part 12th-century priory church which contains some striking monuments to members of the Phelips family.

Stoke-sub-Hamdon
Map 6 ref J10
6 miles NW of Yeovil on the A303

The lanes to the west of Montacute lead to Stoke-sub-Hamdon, another attractive village whose eastern part contains a fine part-Norman church and whose western part contains the remains of a late-medieval priory. The latter was built in the 14th and 15th centuries for the priests of the now-demolished chantry chapel of St Nicholas. The remains, which include an impressive great hall, are now under the ownership of the National Trust. (Open daily, 10am to 6pm, all year round; admission free.)

To the south of the village lies the 400ft **Ham Hill** (or Hamdon Hill), the source of the beautiful honey-coloured building stone of which so many of the surrounding villages are constructed. This solitary limestone outcrop rises abruptly from the Somerset plain providing breathtaking views of the surrounding countryside. A substantial hill fort was sited here during the Iron Age which was subsequently overrun by the ancient Romans. The new occupants built their own fortification here to guard the Fosse Way and its important intersection with the road between Dorchester and the Bristol Channel at nearby Ilchester.

The Romans discovered that Ham Hill's soft even-grained limestone made a flexible and highly attractive building material which was ideal for constructing villas and temples. Later, the Saxons and then the Normans came to share this high opinion of Ham stone, and by the time quarrying reached its height in the 17th century, a sizable settlement had grown up within the boundaries of the old Iron Age fort of which only a solitary inn remains today. A war memorial to 44 local men who died in the First World War stands at the summit of the hill which has now been designated a country park. The combination of the view, the old earthwork ramparts, and maze of overgrown quarry workings make this an outstanding picnic and recreation area.

Tintinhull   Map 6 ref J10
5 miles NW of Yeovil off the A303

Another enchanting National Trust property, **Tintinhull House Garden**, lies in a tranquil position between the A3088, A37 and A303, a couple of miles to the northeast of Ham Hill. Laid out in the early 20th century, the garden is divided by walls and hedges into a series of distinctive areas, each with its own planting theme. These include a pool garden with a delightful lily- and iris-filled pond, a kitchen garden, and a sunken garden which is cleverly designed to give the impression it has many different levels. (Open Wednesdays to Sundays (and Bank Holiday Mondays), 12 noon to 6pm between late-March and late-September.)

The garden is set in the grounds of Tintinhull House, an early 17th-century manor farm to which a spectacular west front was added around 1700. Sadly not open to the public, the house overlooks an attractive triangular green which forms the nucleus of the sprawling village of Tintinhull. A number of other interesting buildings can be seen here, including **Tintinhull Court**, a part-medieval rectory which was remodelled in the 17th and 18th centuries, the Dower House, which was built by the Napper family in 1687, and St Margaret's parish church, a rare example in Somerset of a rectangular single-cell church.

Martock
Map 6 ref J10

7 miles NW of Yeovil on the B3165

The attractive small town of Martock lies on the northern side of the busy A303, two miles west of Tintinhull. Surrounded by fertile arable land, the district has long been renowned for its prosperous land-owning farmers. The community's long-established affluence is reflected in its impressive part 13th-century parish church. A former abbey church which once belonged to the monks of Mont St Michel in Normandy, it boasts one of the finest tie-beams roofs in Somerset, almost every part of which is covered in beautiful carvings.

The old part of Martock contains an unusual number of fine buildings. The National Trust-owned **Treasurer's House** is situated opposite the church. Recently refurbished, this handsome part 13th-century residence incorporates a medieval great hall and cross wing, and a kitchen annexe which was added around 1500. (Open Sundays, Mondays and Tuesdays, 2.30pm to 5.30pm between late March and end-September.) The nearby **Old Court House** is a former parish building which served the locality for 200 years as a grammar school, and to the west, Martock's 17th-century Manor House is the former home of Edward Parker, the man who exposed the Gunpowder Plot after Guy Fawkes had warned him against attending Parliament on the fateful night.

The Somerset Guild of Craftsmen Gallery at Yandles of Martock contains a fascinating range of work made by the county's craftspeople. Items on display include musical instruments, spinning wheels, turned wood, furniture, ceramics, textiles, silver and metalwork. (Open Mondays to Saturdays, 9am to 5pm, all year round.)

East Lambrook
Map 6 ref I10

8 miles NW of Yeovil off the B3165

The lanes to the west of Martock lead to the charming hamlet of East Lambrook, home of the beautiful **East Lambrook Manor Garden**. The garden was laid out by the writer and horticulturalist, Margery Fish, who lived at the medieval Ham-stone manor from 1937 until her death in 1969. Her exuberant planting and deliberate lack of formality created an atmosphere of romantic tranquillity which is maintained to this day. Now Grade I listed, the story of the genesis of the project is told in her first book, *"We Made A Garden"*. The National Collection of cranesbill species geraniums is also kept here. (Open Mondays to Saturdays, 10am to 5pm between 1 March and 31 October.)

The low-lying land to the north of East Lambrook is crisscrossed by a network of drainage ditches, or rhines (pronounced reens), which eventually flow into the rivers Parrett, Isle and Yeo. Originally cut in the early 1800s, the ditches are often lined with double rows of pollarded willows which have come to characterise this part of Somerset. Despite having to be cleared every few years, the rhines provide a valuable natural habitat for a wide variety of bird, animal and plantlife.

An interesting way to discover more about this unique wetlands environment is to call in at the ***Thorney Moor Farm Park*** which is located between East Lambrook and the village of Muchelney. (Open Tuesdays to Sundays, 10am to 6pm between early-March and end-October.) Also located nearby is the thatched workshop of the potter, John Leach, whose grandfather, Bernard, established the famous Leach Pottery at St Ives in Cornwall in the 1920s. (Open Mondays to Saturdays, 9am to 5pm (1pm Saturdays), all year round.)

Somerton to Wincanton

Somerton   *Map 6 ref J9*
10 miles N of Yeovil on the B3153

The B3153 to the east of Langport leads to Somerton, a fine old town which was the capital of Somerset for a time under the West Saxons. The settlement grew up around an important crossroads to the northwest of the church. However, an expansion towards the end of the 13th century altered the original layout and created the present open market place with its distinctive ***Market Cross*** and town hall, both later additions. Between 1278 and 1371, Somerton became the location of the county gaol and meeting place of the shire courts. It also continued to develop as a market town, a role which is reflected in such delightfully down-to-earth street names as Cow Square and Pig Street (now Broad Street).

Present-day Somerton is filled with handsome old shops, inns and houses, the majority of which are constructed of local bluish lias limestone. The general atmosphere of mature prosperity is enhanced by the presence of a number of striking early buildings. These include the 17th-century ***Hext Almshouses*** and the part 13th-

Somerton Market Cross, Somerton

century church with its magnificent 15th-century tie-beam roof and unusual transeptal south tower.

Muchelney   *Map 6 ref I10*
4 miles SW of Somerton off the A372

Muchelney is the location of an impressive part-ruined Benedictine monastery which was founded in Saxon times around 950. During the medieval period, ***Muchelney Abbey*** grew to emulate its great rival at Glastonbury; however, after the Dissolution of the Monasteries in 1539, the building gradually fell into disrepair and much of its stone was removed to provide building material for the surrounding village. In spite of this, a substantial part of the original structure remains, including the south cloister and abbot's lodge. Now under the custodianship of English Heritage, the abbey is open daily, 10am to 6pm between 1 April and 30 September. An exhibition of pottery by John Leach and furniture by Stuart Interiors can be seen in the abbey grounds.

Muchelney's parish church is worth seeing for its remarkable early 17th-century illuminations on the ceiling of the nave. Opposite stands the ***Priest's House***, a late-medieval hall house with large Gothic windows which was originally a residence for priests serving at the church across the road. This has recently been refurbished by the National Trust and is open Sundays and Mondays only, 2.30pm to 5.30pm between late March and late September.

Drayton
Map 6 ref I10

5 miles SW of Somerton off the A378

The privately-owned **Midelney Manor** can be found at Drayton, a mile and a half to the west. Originally an island manor belonging to the abbots of Muchelney, this handsome 16th to 18th-century manor house has been owned by the Trevilian family since the early 1500s. The estate incorporates a heronry, a series of delightful gardens and woodland walks, and the unique 17th-century Falcons Mews. (Open Thursdays and Bank Holiday Mondays, 2.30pm to 5.30pm between late April and end-September.)

Curry Rivel
Map 6 ref I10

7 miles SW of Somerton on the A378

One of the oldest and most atmospheric pubs in the area can be found in the village of Curry Rivel, one and a half miles to the west of Drayton on the A378 Taunton-Langport road. **The Old Forge Inn** is a handsome 14th-century free house which is thought to have monastic origins. One of its doorways, which is now sealed off, is reputed to have led to a nearby monastery via a secret passage. Now extensively modernised, the interior retains great charm and now features a permanent exhibition of work by the artist E R Sturgeon.

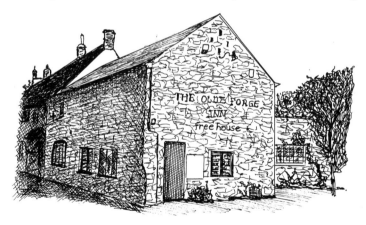

Old Forge Inn

A fine range ales and light meals is served throughout the inn, and the traditionally-furnished restaurant, which is a no-smoking area, offers an excellent menu catering for all tastes including vegetarian. A succulent carvery is a further option, and the extensive wine list offers a choice of carefully-selected and sensibly-priced wines from around the world. The Cellar Bar has a fine vaulted ceiling and is ideal for small parties and meetings, being private yet adjacent to the restaurant and public bar. The room was only discovered some 25 years ago during renovations when one of the old beams crashed through the floor. The Old Forge has a small landscaped beer garden and ample parking, and is an excellent choice for those seeking a fine country pub. *Old Forge Inn, Church Street, Curry Rivel, Somerset Tel: 01485 251554*

Langport
Map 6 ref I9

5 miles W of Somerton on the A378

The small former market town of Langport lies three miles along the A378 to the northeast of Curry Rivel. The old part of the town stands on a rise above an ancient fording point on the River Parrett, a short distance downstream from where it is joined by the rivers Isle and Yeo. Defended by an earthwork rampart during Saxon times, by 930 it was an important commercial centre which minted its own coins. The town's surviving east gate incorporates a curious *"hanging"* chapel which sits above the arch on an upper level. The tower at Huish Episcopi can be seen through its barrel-vaulted gateway. Langport's own parish church is worth a look for its beautiful stained-glass windows and finely-carved 12th-century lintel over the south doorway.

During the 18th and 19th centuries, Langport flourished as a banking centre, and the local independent bank, Stuckey's, became known for their impressive branches, many of which can still be seen in the surrounding towns and villages trading under the banner of NatWest. At the time of its amalgamation in 1909, Stuckey's had more notes in circulation than any other in the country except the Bank of England.

Throughout history, the Langport Gap has been the site of a number of important military encounters. Two of the most significant occurred over 1000 years apart: the first involved Geraint, King of the Dumnonii in the 6th century, and the second, the Battle of Langport of July 1645, gave Parliament almost total control of the South West during the English Civil War.

Huish Episcopi
Map 6 ref I9

5 miles SW of Somerton on the A372

One of the finest examples in the county of a late-medieval *"Somerset"* tower can be found on the church at Huish Episcopi, an ancient community which almost adjoins Langport to the southeast. At its most impressive in high summer when viewed through the surrounding greenery, this ornate honey-brown structure is adorned with striking tracery, pinnacles and carvings. The church also possesses an elaborate Norman doorway, which shows signs of having been affected by the fire that destroyed much of the earlier building in the 13th century, and a window in the south chapel which was designed by the 19th-century Pre-Raphaelite, Edward Burne-Jones.

Aller
Map 6 ref I9
5 miles W of Somerton on the A372

Another historic event occurred in the church at Aller, two miles along the A372 Bridgwater road to the northwest of Langport. It was here in 878 AD that King Alfred converted Guthrum the Dane and his followers to Christianity following a battle on Salisbury Plain. The low wooded rise to the east of Aller is crisscrossed by a network of ancient country lanes. These connect some pleasant hamlets and villages, among them High Ham, the location of the last thatched windmill in England. Dating from 1822 and remaining in use until 1910, the **Stembridge Tower Mill** is now under the ownership of the National Trust. (Open Sundays, Mondays and Wednesdays, 2pm to 5pm between late March and end-September.)

Kingsdon
Map 6 ref J9
3 miles SE of Somerton off the B3151

The B3151 to the southeast of Somerton leads to the village of Kingsdon, a mile to the east of which lies the delightful National Trust-owned country house and garden of **Lytes Cary**. This late-medieval manor house was built by succeeding generations of the Lyte family, the best-known member of which is Henry Lyte, the Elizabethan horticulturalist who translated Dodoen's Cruydeboeck from the Dutch to create the celebrated work of reference known as Lyte's Herbal. Dedicated to the Queen, it went on to be reprinted several times as an interest in physic gardening began to develop. The present garden is an enchanting combination of formality and eccentricity: there is an open lawn lined with magnificent yew topiary, an orchard filled with quince, pear and apple trees, and a network of enclosed paths which every now and then reveal a view of the house, a lily-pond or a classical statue. The house was built over a long period and incorporates a 14th-century chapel, a 15th-century hall and a 16th-century great chamber. (Open Mondays, Wednesdays and Saturdays, 2pm to 6pm between late-March and late-October.)

Ilchester
Map 6 ref K10

5 miles SE of Somerton off the B3151

To the south of Lytes Cary, the B3151 crosses the A303 before arriving in Ilchester, a pleasant, if unexceptional, small town which, like Somerton, is a former county town. In Roman times, the settlement stood at the point where the north-south route between Dorchester and the Bristol Channel crossed the Fosse Way. However, it was during the 13th century that the town reached its peak as a centre of administration, agriculture and learning. Ilchester rose to become the county town of Somerset and three substantial gaols were built here, one of which remained in use until the 1840s. Another indication of its former status, a 13th-century mace thought to be the oldest staff of office in England, can still be seen in the town hall.

Roger Bacon, the celebrated scholar, monk and scientist, was born in Ilchester around 1214. He went on to predict the invention of the aeroplane, telescope and steam engine, and was eventually confined for his outspoken ideas. No doubt he would be quietly satisfied by the existence of the aircraft museum at nearby Yeovilton if he were alive today.

Today, the town is bypassed by the A303 east-west trunk route and most of the worries of the outside world. The tiny **Ilchester Museum** can be found in the centre of town by the Market Cross. The museum tells the story of Ilchester from pre-Roman times to the 20th century. Exhibits include a Roman coffin and skeleton, and a series of displays describing Ilchester's past as a country town. (Open Thursdays and Saturdays between May and September.)

Yeovilton
Map 6 ref K10

5 miles SE of Somerton off the B3151

One of the world's leading aviation museums is situated on the B3151 three miles to the east of Ilchester. **The Fleet Air Arm Museum** at Yeovilton contains a unique collection of over 80 aircraft, around half of which are on permanent display. There is also an impressive series of exhibits illustrating the history of naval aviation from 1910 to the present day. Special displays include those on World Wars I and II, kamikaze warfare, the Korean War, the Harrier Jump Jet and Concorde. There is also a helicopter simulator and the *"Ultimate Carrier Experience"*, a large and complex exhibit consisting of a flight deck with steam catapult, deck landing site, and eleven carrier-borne aircraft. In addition, there are displays of weapons, medals and memorabilia which bring to life the exciting world of naval aviation and the people who have been part of it. (Open daily, 10am to 5.30pm (4.30pm in winter), all year round.)

Sparkford *Map 6 ref K9*
7 miles E of Somerton on the A303
Another interesting museum can be found on the northeastern edge of Sparkford, five miles to the east of Yeovilton. Situated beside the A359 near its junction with the A303, the **Haynes Motor Museum** is a unique collection of over 200 veteran, vintage and classic cars and motorbikes which is thought to be the largest of its kind in the UK. Nearly every exhibit is driven at least once every six months around a specially-constructed one-kilometre demonstration track. Special displays include Jaguars, Minis, Chevrolet Corvettes and red-painted sports cars. (Open daily, 9.30am to 5.30pm (10am to 4pm in winter), all year round.)

Cadbury Castle *Map 6 ref K9*
7 miles W of Wincanton off the A303
Halfway between Ilchester and Wincanton, the A303 passes along the northern edge of **Cadbury Castle**, a massive Iron Age hill fort which is also reckoned by some to be the location of King Arthur's legendary Camelot. This ancient hilltop site was occupied for some 5000 years from the middle to the Neolithic period right up to the 13th century. Heavily fortified throughout the Iron Age, the Romans are reputed to have carried out a massacre here around 70 AD to put down a revolt by the ancient Britons. A major archeological excavation in the 1960s uncovered a wealth of Roman and pre-Roman remains on the site. It also confirmed the existence of a substantial fortification dating from around 500 AD, the time when King Arthur would have been spearheading the Celtic-British resistance against the advancing Saxons. If Cadbury Castle had indeed been Arthur's Camelot, it is likely that it would have been a timber fortification and not the turreted stone structure mythologised by the storybooks.

The easily-defended hilltop site was again refortified during the reign of Ethelred the Unready, this time against the Danes. The poorly-advised king also established a mint here around 1000 AD, most of the coinage from which was used to buy off the Norse invaders in an act of appeasement which led to the term Danegeld. As a consequence, most of the surviving coins from the Cadbury mint are now to be found in the museums of Scandinavia.

The mile-long stroll around Cadbury Castle's massive earthwork ramparts demonstrates the site's effectiveness as a defensive position. Thanks to the magnificent view from the top, troop movements to the north and west would have been easily spotted, and the important route into the Heart of England, the Fosse Way, would have been clearly visible five miles away to the northwest.

Another exceptional view of south Somerset can be had from the summit of **Corton Hill**, two miles to the south. The site of an ancient beacon, it can be reached by following Halter Path Lane from the village of Corton Denham.

Templecombe   *Map 7 ref M10*
5 miles S of Wincanton on the A357

To the east of Corton Hill, the unusual **Gartell Light Railway** runs through the beautiful swathe of countryside known as Blackmore Vale. Situated near the village of Templecombe, this rare 2ft gauge line currently runs for almost a mile along the trackbed of the much-loved Somerset and Dorset Railway which was closed over thirty years ago. Trains run every fifteen minutes from Common Lane station, which also has a visitor centre, refreshment room and shop. The nearby **Templecombe Railway Museum** houses a fascinating display of artefacts, photographs and models which tell the story of nearby Templecombe station, once a busy junction where some 130 railwaymen were employed. Telephone 01963 370752 for information on open days.

Wincanton   *Map 7 ref L9*
12 miles NE of Yeovil on the A303

The A337 to the north of Templecombe leads to the old cloth-making centre of Wincanton. This pleasant former coaching town lies almost exactly half way between London and the long-established naval base at Plymouth, and in the heyday of the horse-drawn carriage, up to twenty coaches a day would stop here. At that time the inns could provide lodging for scores of travellers and stabling for over 250 horses. The old sector stands on a draughty hillside above the River Cale. It still contains a surprising number of fine Georgian buildings, some of which were constructed to replace earlier ones destroyed in a town fire in 1747. Apart from the medieval carving of St Eligius in the north porch, the parish church is a Victorian rebuild which only merits a brief look.

Modern Wincanton is a peaceful light industrial town whose best-known attraction is probably its **National Hunt Racecourse**. Horse racing began in the locality in the 18th century and moved to its present site to the north of the town centre in 1927. Regular meetings are held here between October and May, or for golfing enthusiasts, the racecourse incorporates a challenging nine hole pay and play course which is open throughout the year. Also worth visiting is the beautiful **Hadspen House Garden**, which is situated beside the A371 Shepton Mallet road, four miles to the northwest of Wincanton.

Castle Cary
Map 7 ref L9
7 miles NE of Wincanton on the A371

Castle Cary District Museum, Castle Cary

The lovely little town of Castle Cary lies to the west of this road, a couple of miles further on. Once the site of an impressive Norman castle, this has all but disappeared and today, the town has the atmosphere of mature rural calm. The streets contain a number of exceptional old buildings, including the handsome 18th-century post office and distinctive beehive-shaped lock-up gaol which dates from the 1770s. The **Castle Cary District Museum** occupies the splendid Market House in the centre of the town. Largely constructed in 1855, the building incorporates a magnificent 17th-century colonnade. (Open daily between April and September.) The rectory at Ansford, on the northern edge of Castle Cary, is the former home of the 18th-century diarist, James Woodforde, whose life seemed to have revolved around the consumption of lavish meals.

Bruton
Map 7 ref L8
5 miles N of Wincanton on the A359
The remarkably well-preserved former clothing and ecclesiastical centre of Bruton lies on the A359, three miles to the northeast of Castle Cary. More a small town than a village, a priory was

established here in the 11th century on the south side of the River Brue. The former priory **Church of St Mary** is a fine Perpendicular structure with a soaring 100ft west tower. It also has a rare secondary tower which was built over the north porch in the late 14th century. The church interior is unusually light and spacious, and contains a number of memorials to the Berkeley family, the local lords of the manor who also owned the land on which London's Berkeley Square now stands.

A walk around the streets of Bruton reveals some interesting historic features. The curious square structure across the river from the church is the **Patwell Pump**, a communal parish water pump which remained in use until the early 20th century, and a little further downstream, a 15th-century arched packhorse bridge can be seen near the site of the famous part 16th-century King's School. Perhaps Bruton's most distinctive building, **The Dovecote**, can be seen on the crest of a hill to the south of here. Built in the 15th century, it is thought to have doubled as a watch tower and is now under the custodianship of the National Trust.

Among the many fine buildings to be seen in Bruton High Street are the Pharmacy, with its elegant 18th-century facade, and the intriguingly-named **Sexey's Hospital**, a 17th-century almshouse which was founded by Elizabeth I's auditor, Hugh Sexey.

The delightful, family-owned **Claire-De-Lune Restaurant** can be found at the end of the High Street in the heart of this attractive small town. The proprietors, Sandie and Keith Lockyer, are charming hosts who provide the warmest of welcomes. They are assisted by their daughter, Michelle, whose husband and chef, Phil Hartley, trained in the provinces, then worked in London and provincial hotels before becoming head chef at the four-star Carlton Hotel in Great Yarmouth; latterly he has worked in other hotels and for Anglia Television.

Serving both a la carte and table d'hote menus, this impressive restaurant offers a wide variety of English dishes, all of which are cooked to order using fresh local produce. A specially selected wine-of-the-month adds the finishing touch. On Sundays, traditional lunch has become so popular that prior booking is strongly recommended. Rated three crowns by the English Tourist Board, the Claire-De-Lune has an attractive function suite and is pleased to cater for small parties. For those wishing to stay over, a comfortable double en suite guest room is also available. *Claire-De-Lune Restaurant, 2-4 High Street, Bruton, Somerset   Tel: 01749 813395*

Claire-De-Lune Restaurant

Stourhead

Map 7 ref N8

6 miles NE of Wincanton off the B3092

For those keen to explore this beautiful part of Somerset on foot, the **Leland Trail** long-distance footpath starts at King Alfred's Tower on the glorious National Trust-owned **Stourhead Estate**, six miles to the east of Bruton. The 25-mile trail passes through the wooded hills and valleys of Camelot country and takes in Bruton, Castle Cary, Cadbury Castle and Tintinhull on its way to Ham Hill. A further long-distance footpath, the **Liberty Trail**, then continues southwestwards through the Ham-stone country of south Somerset and finally passes out of the county near **Forde Abbey**.

CHAPTER SIX
West Somerset and Exmoor

Packhorse Bridge, Allerford

6
West Somerset and Exmoor

Bridgwater

The ancient inland port and industrial town of Bridgwater stands at the lowest medieval bridging point on the River Parrett. Despite having been fortified since before the Norman invasion, the settlement remained little more than a village until an international trade in wool, wheat and other agricultural produce began to develop in the late Middle Ages. During this period, Bridgwater grew to become the most important town on the coast between Bristol and Barnstaple, and the fifth-busiest port in Britain. The largely 14th-century parish **Church of St Mary**, with its disproportionately large spire, is the only building to survive from this medieval era of prosperity, the castle having been dismantled after the English Civil War, and the 13th-century Franciscan friary and St John's hospital having long since disappeared. The oldest and most interesting part of the town lies between King Street and the West Quay, an area whose layout is medieval, but whose buildings are amongst the finest examples of Georgian domestic architecture in Somerset.

Prior to the construction of a canal dock a short distance downstream early in the 19th century, ships used to tie up on both riverbanks below Bridgwater's medieval three-arched bridge. The last remnant of the castle, *The Water Gate*, can still be seen here on the West Quay, along with a number of fine Georgian residences, the most notable of which, the Lions, was built in 1725.

After a long period of decline brought about by a long-running war with the nation's continental trading partners, Bridgwater underwent something of an industrial renaissance during the first half of the 19th century. The manufacture of Bridgwater glass, which had begun the previous century, continued to expand, and a canal terminus, complete with docks, warehouses, brickworks and retractable railway bridge, was built between 1837 and 1841 a few hundred yards north of the old centre. Finally closed in 1970, the site has been restored and is now a fascinating piece of industrial archeology which is well worth seeing. Bridgwater's manufacturers have long since relocated to the outskirts of town. The most evident of these, a cellophane factory, makes its presence known to residents and visitors alike by its distinctive airborne aroma.

The interior of the parish church is worth seeing for its painting of the Descent from the Cross by an unknown Italian artist, and for the fine Jacobean screen which extends across a side chapel. It was from the church tower that the Duke of Monmouth is reputed to have spotted the approaching army of James II the day before the Battle of Sedgemoor. This supposed advantage gave him the inspiration to launch the surprise attack which eventually led to his disastrous defeat in July 1685.

River Parrett Inn

When in Bridgwater, it is well worth making the effort to find the **River Parrett Inn**, an attractive traditional pub and eating place which enjoys a delightful aspect overlooking the river in Salmon Parade. Easy to reach from junction 24 on the M5, it makes a pleasant stopping-off point when travelling to or from Exmoor or the west Somerset coast. Proprietors Louise and Mark Pearce have successfully created a relaxed and friendly atmosphere which is welcoming to visitors and locals alike. They serve an impressive range of traditional ales and are renowned throughout the locality for their food.

The menu features a mixture of well-known dishes, including scampi, chilli con carne and jacket potatoes, along with a choice of more adventurous items, such as chicken and broccoli bake. Vegetarians are well catered for and there is also a chalkboard offering a range of daily specials, which on the day we visited included fisherman's pie and mushroom and nut fettucini. Children are most welcome, and the menu features a number of items which are especially suitable for younger diners. The Parrett Inn also offers an impressive range of traditional pub games, including darts, pool, skittles and shove ha'penny. *River Parrett Inn, Salmon Parade, Bridgwater, Somerset Tel: 01278 459013*

A bronze statue of Bridgwater's most famous son, Robert Blake, can be seen at the top of Fore Street. This celebrated military leader was born in 1598 in the house which now accommodates **Bridgwater's Town Museum.** When in his forties, Blake became an important officer in Cromwell's army and twice defended Taunton against overwhelming Royalist odds, then at the age of fifty, he was given command of the British navy and went on to win a number of important battles against the Dutch and Spanish, so restoring the nation's naval supremacy in Europe. The museum contains a three-dimensional model of the Battle of Santa Cruz, one of his most famous victories, along with a collection of his personal effects.

There is also a similar diorama of the Battle of Sedgemoor and a large collection of locally-discovered artefacts dating from the Neolithic period to the Second World War. (Open daily, 11am (2pm Sundays) to 5pm, all year round.) Also well worth seeing is Bridgwater's spectacular annual carnival which is held in the town on the first Thursday in November.

Bridgwater to the Quantock Hills

Durleigh   *Map 1 ref H8*
2 miles W of Bridgwater off the A39
At Durleigh, in the lanes two miles to the west of Bridgwater, **West Bower Farm** is an extraordinary building which incorporates a twin-turreted medieval gatehouse. The nearby reservoir, which offers good freshwater fishing, is fed by the Bridgwater and Taunton Canal.

Enmore

Map 1 ref G8

4 miles W of Bridgwater off the A39

Continuing westwards to the village of Enmore, the small redbrick country mansion of **Barford Park** can be found on the road to Four Forks. This delightfully-proportioned Queen Anne house is set in extensive grounds incorporating a walled flower garden, a water garden, an archery glade and a large area of broad-leafed woodland. The interior contains some exceptional examples of Queen Anne furniture and is still in daily family use. (Open by appointment only; telephone 01278 671269.)

To the west of Enmore, the ground rises into the Quantock Hills, an *"Area of Outstanding Natural Beauty"* which stretches from Kingston St Mary in the south to Quantoxhead on the Bristol Channel coast. Rising to a highest point of 1260ft at Wills Neck near Crowcombe, this delightful area of open heath and scattered woodland supports one of the country's last remaining herds of wild red deer. The exposed hilltops are littered with Neolithic and Bronze Age remains, including around a hundred burial mounds, many of which now resemble simple piles of stones. The richer soil to the south sustains arable farms and pockets of dense woodland. This varied landscape, several tracts of which are owned by the National Trust, offers some excellent opportunities for walking and riding.

Broomfield

Map 1 ref G9

5 miles SW of Bridgwater off the A38

One of the loveliest areas in the southern Quantocks can be found in the lanes to the south of Enmore around the village of Broomfield. This is the location of **Fyne Court**, the headquarters of the Somerset Trust for Nature Conservation. Leased to the organisation by the National Trust, the 26-acre grounds are a designated nature reserve which incorporates a walled garden, two ponds, a lake and a small arboretum. The main house was built in the 17th century by the Crosse family but was largely destroyed by fire in the 1890s. The only parts to survive were the library and music room, and these have now been converted into an impressive interpretation centre and eating place which are open daily, 9am to 6pm, all year round; admission free.

The most renowned occupant of Fyne Court, Andrew Crosse, was an early 19th-century scientist who was a pioneer in the field of electrical energy. Known locally as *"the thunder and lightning man"*, one of his lightning conductors can still be seen on an oak tree in the grounds. Rumour has it that during one of his experiments, Crosse created tiny live insects, a claim which helped inspire Mary Shelley to write her Gothic horror story, Frankenstein, in 1818.

Nether Stowey

Map 1 ref G8

6 miles W of Bridgwater on the A39

Around the turn of the 19th century, the beautiful upland landscape to the west of Bridgwater became a favourite retreat for novelists and poets of the Romantic movement. Nether Stowey is a peaceful village on the northwestern edge of the Quantocks which thankfully is now bypassed by the main A39 Bridgwater to Minehead road. In 1797, a local tanner, Tom Poole, lent a cottage at the end of his garden to his friend, Samuel Taylor Coleridge, who stayed there for three years with his wife and child. During this time he wrote *"The Rime Of The Ancient Mariner"* and sections of *"Christabel and Frost At Midnight"*.

Coleridge was visited on a number of occasions by such literary luminaries of the day as William Wordsworth and Charles Lamb in a colourful invasion which is claimed to have led the locals to believe they were harbouring a den of French spies. *Coleridge's Cottage* is now owned by the National Trust and is open to visitors on Sundays, Tuesdays, Wednesdays and Thursdays, 2pm to 5pm between late-March and end-September. Coleridge and his friends are rumoured to have drunk at the 400 year-old Castle of Comfort Inn at nearby Dodington.

In Norman times, Nether Stowey was the site of an early motte and bailey castle, the foundations of which can still be seen on the hill to the west of the present-day centre. A substantial manor house, *Stowey Court*, stands at the opposite end of the village. This was begun by Lord Audley in 1497 shortly before he joined a protest against Henry VII's taxation policy. Sadly, he wasn't able to see the project through to completion as he was executed soon after. The clock tower in the centre of Nether Stowey was erected in 1897 to replace a medieval market cross, a reminder that this was once a small market town.

Over Stowey

Map 1 ref G8

6 miles W of Bridgwater off the A39

A lane to the south of Nether Stowey rises up towards Over Stowey, the starting point of the Forestry Commission's *Quantock Forest Trail*. This pleasant three-mile walk is lined with specially-planted native and imported trees, most of which have been introduced since World War II. To the northwest of Nether Stowey, *Dodington Hall* is a small privately-owned manor house which is only open to visitors for a few days each year. A Tudor gem set in attractive semi-formal gardens, its great hall features a splendid oak roof and a carved stone fireplace. (Open Sundays only, 2pm to 5pm between mid-May and late-July.)

Holford
Map 5 ref F7

8 miles W of Bridgwater on the A39

Continuing westwards, the A39 connects a number of charming rural settlements, many of which provide access to the wooded combes and bracken-covered hillsides of the Quantocks. A track from the village of Holford leads up to a large Iron Age hill fortification known as **Dowsborough Fort**. A little further west, two of the most dramatic viewpoints in the Quantocks, **Beacon Hill** and **Bicknoller Hill**, lie on National Trust-owned land overlooking the Bristol Channel and the Vale of Taunton Deane. On the latter can be seen an Iron Age livestock enclosure known as **Trendle Ring**, now an ancient monument. The view to the northeast takes in the angular shape of the Hinkley Point nuclear power station on the coast.

Stogursey
Map 5 ref G7

6 miles NW of Bridgwater off the A39

The ancient village of Stogursey lies midway between Nether Stowey and the Bristol Channel. In the 12th century, this was the lair of the renegade lord, Fulke de Breaute, who along with a band of ruthless followers, terrorised the surrounding population until he was hunted down and brought to justice. The remains of his castle can still be made out near the village.

Kilve
Map 5 ref F7

9 miles W of Bridgwater on the A39

At Kilve, on the A39 three miles to the west, there is a delightful little church with a squat medieval-looking tower. This is thought to date from the 17th century as prior to 1636, the church bells were housed in a wooden structure in the churchyard. The nearby ruins are the remains of a medieval chantry, or college of priests, whose chapel stood to the north of the present church.

A track beyond the churchyard leads down to a boulder-strewn beach, an agreeable place despite its reputation as a favoured haunt of glats, conger eels up to ten feet in length which are known to lie in wait among the rocks near the shore. Once known as "*St Keyna's serpents*", local people used to search for them using trained "*fish dogs*".

East Quantoxhead
Map 5 ref F7

10 miles W of Bridgwater off the A39

From Kilve, a pleasant walk to the northwest leads to East

Quantoxhead, a picturesque village containing a delightful assortment of thatched cottages, a mill with a millpond, and a handsome old manor house, ***Court House***, which stands within a beautiful garden on a rise overlooking the sea. The owner's family bloodline can be traced back to the time of the Domesday Book. In the 13th century, the manor passed by marriage to the Luttrells, the subsequent owners of Dunster Castle, and in the 16th and 17th centuries the present house was constructed by successive generations of the same family. The church beside the house is a fine example of a late medieval estate church. Inside, there is some fine Renaissance woodwork, an imposing chest tomb commemorating two 16th-century members of the Luttrell family, and a rare 14th-century rood screen, one of only a handful in Somerset.

West Quantoxhead   *Map 5 ref F7*
12 miles W of Bridgwater on the A39
Little remains of the village of West Quantoxhead, or St Audrie's, two miles to the west, following an extensive redevelopment in the mid 19th century. Its principal features are a Victorian mansion, now a girls' school, a handsome neo-Gothic church, and a series of unusual gates, fences and walls which create an impression of organised rural respectability.

Steart   *Map 5 ref H7*
6 miles NW of Bridgwater on the Coast
The stretch coastline between Quantoxhead and the ***Bird Sanctuary*** near Steart, ten miles to the east, is for the most part bleak and uninteresting. The sanctuary is located on the low peninsula between the Parrett estuary and the Bristol Channel, and from here is it possible to view the fast-flowing offshore tidal race, a dramatic and dangerous spectacle. From Steart, there is a footpath along the west bank of the Parrett all the way to Bridgwater. Places of interest along the way include Combwich, once the lowest fording point on the river and the likely site of a great battle between the Saxons and the Danes, and Chilton Trinity, a village with a fine church which can be reached by taking a shortcut avoiding a major bend in the river. On the A39 three miles to the west of Bridgwater, the ***Heritage Gardens at Cannington College*** contain an impressive collection of rare and exotic plants, a selection of which are for sale in the specialist plant centre. (Open daily, 2pm to 5pm between Easter and end-October.)

Taunton

Taunton, the county town of Somerset, has only been its sole centre of administration since 1936, previous county towns having been Ilchester and Somerton. The settlement was founded as a military camp by the Saxon King Ine in the 8th century, and by Norman times it had grown to have its own Augustinian monastery, minster and castle. An extensive structure whose purpose has always been more administrative than military, the castle was nevertheless the focus of two important sieges during the English Civil War. A few years later, over 150 followers of the Duke of Monmouth were sentenced to death here by the infamous Judge Jeffreys during the Bloody Autumn Assizes which followed the Pitchfork Rebellion of 1685. Even now, the judge's ghost is said to haunt the castle grounds on September nights.

Somerset County Cricket Museum, Taunton

Today, the much-altered castle houses the **Somerset County Museum**, an informative local museum containing a large collection of exhibits on the archeology and natural history of the county. There is also a special display chronicling the colourful history of the Somerset Light Infantry. (Open Mondays to Saturdays, 10am to 5pm, all year round.)

Somerset's famous County Cricket Ground occupies part of the old priory grounds which once stretched down to the river. A section of the old monastic gatehouse known as the Priory Barn can still be seen beside the cricket ground. Now restored, this medieval stone building now houses the fascinating **Somerset County Cricket Museum**.

In common with many other towns and villages in the West Country, Taunton was a thriving wool, cloth-making, and later silk, centre during the late Middle Ages. The profits earned by the medieval clothiers went to build not one, but two huge churches: St James' and St Mary's. Both have soaring Perpendicular towers, which have since been rebuilt, and imposing interiors; the former contains a striking carved stone font and the latter an elegant painted roof adorned with angels. The town centre is scattered with other fine buildings, most notably the timber-framed Tudor House in Fore Street and the 17th-century almshouses.

Present-day Taunton continues to be an important commercial centre with a lively weekly market and a thriving light industrial sector which benefits from some excellent transport links with the rest of the country. Other visitor attractions include **Vivary Park**, with its ponds, gardens and jogging trail, and the impressive **Brewhouse Theatre and Arts Centre**. This was opened in 1977 after a concerted fund-raising effort by townspeople interested in the arts who felt that the county town of Taunton should have its own theatre. The modern auditorium seats 350 and the adjoining administration offices are housed in a handsome Grade II listed building. The centre offers a full programme of theatre, music, dance, cabaret and children's shows, and there is also a studio, an art gallery and a popular restaurant and bar.

A pleasant walk follows the towpath of the **Bridgwater and Taunton Canal**, a 14 mile inland waterway which was constructed in the 1820s and fully reopened in the summer of 1994 following decades of neglect and a 20 year programme of restoration. A relative latecomer when it first opened in 1827, the canal was constructed as part of an ambitious scheme to create a freight route between Exeter and Bristol which avoided the treacherous journey around the Cornish peninsula. For many years, the canal was the principal means of importing coal and iron from South Wales to the towns of inland Somerset, and of exporting wool and agricultural produce to the urban centres of Britain.

The towpath winds its way through some of the most attractive countryside in the Somerset Levels, and the restored locks, swing bridges, engine houses and rare paddle-gearing equipment add interest to the walk. The canal also offers a variety of recreational facilities, including boating, fishing, canoeing and bird watching, and passes close to some attractive villages. At North Newton, there is a small country manor, **Maunsel House**, which is occasionally open to visitors, and at Creech St Michael, there is a part 13th-century church which is worth seeing for its fine wagon roof. At the canal's southern end, boats have access to the River Tone via **Firepool Lock** in the heart of Taunton.

Vale of Taunton Deane

Cheddon Fitzpaine
Map 5 ref G9
2 miles N of Taunton off the A38

In the lanes to the north of Taunton town centre, the beautiful **Hestercombe Gardens** lie on the south-facing foothills of the Quantocks just north of the village of Cheddon Fitzpaine. This carefully-restored Edwardian garden is an outstanding example of the professional collaboration between the architect, Sir Edwin Lutyens, and the landscape designer, Gertrude Jekyll. Originally laid out in 1904, Hestercombe was restored in the 1980s by Somerset County Council using Jekyll's original planting scheme as a guide. (Open daily, 9am (2pm weekends) to 5pm, all year round; closed weekends in winter.)

Bishops Lydeard
Map 5 ref F9
3 miles NW of Taunton on the A358

The sizable village of Bishops Lydeard lies four miles west of Hestercombe Gardens, off the A358 Williton road. This is the southern terminus of the **West Somerset Railway**, a privately-operated steam railway which runs for almost twenty miles to Minehead on the Bristol Channel coast. The longest line of its kind in the country, it was formed when British Rail's 100-year-old branch between Taunton and Minehead was closed in 1971. After a five-year restoration programme, the new company began operating a limited summer service which has steadily grown in popularity. Special attractions include the first class Pullman dining car and the *"Flockton Flyer"*, a steam locomotive which may be recognised for its many appearances on film and television. Services between the line's ten stations run throughout the day between mid-March and end-October.

Norton Fitzwarren
Map 5 ref G9
2 miles W of Taunton off the B3227

Farmhouse cider has been made in the countryside around Taunton since the first professional cider-makers came over from Normandy with William the Conqueror. The damp fertile land in this part of Somerset is ideal for growing cider apples, and a number of producers, large and small, continue to operate in the area. One of the largest has its factory at Norton Fitzwarren, a scattered village on the B3227, a couple of miles west of Taunton. The remains of an early Bronze Age bank and ditch enclosure can also be made out here, artefacts from which can be seen in the county museum at Taunton Castle.

Bradford-on-Tone   *Map 5 ref F10*
3 miles SW of Taunton off the A38

A fascinating few hours can be spent at **Sheppy's Cider Farm Centre** at Bradford-on-Tone, a unique visitor attraction which lies beside the A38 midway between Taunton and Wellington, only two miles from junction 26 on the M5. Since the Sheppy family began making traditional cider here in 1925 they have won over 200 awards for their quality ciders, including two gold medals at the Brewer's Exhibition. A large part of the farm continues to be given over to cider orchards where apples are cultivated with such romantic names as Tremlett's Bitter, Yarlington Mill, Dabinett and the famous Kingston Black.

Sheppy's Cider

Richard and Mary Sheppy, and their son David, are proud to keep alive the ancient Somerset craft of cider-making, and in recent years, they have taken important steps to widen their range of ciders and improve marketing. The Cider Farm Centre has also been much improved to include such attractions as a farm and cider museum, a video presentation of the cider-maker's year, children's play area, picnic area and nature walks; a licensed tearoom is also open between May and October. Visitors are welcome throughout the year, with casual guided tours of the orchards and cellars being available from May to October (please telephone for times). Pre-booked group visits can be arranged between April and Christmas, and there is also a well-stocked farm shop offering customers the opportunity to taste before they buy. *Sheppy's Cider, Three Bridges, Bradford-on-Tone, Taunton, Somerset   Tel: 01823 461233   Fax: 01823 461712*

Westbuckland
Map 5 ref G10

3 miles SW of Taunton off the A38

Situated in the hamlet of Westbuckland near junction 26 on the M5, the very popular **Blackbird Inn** can be found off the A38 midway between Taunton and Wellington. The building has had a long and interesting past: a certain Edward Richards is known to have drawn ale here in 1775, and there is also evidence supporting a much older history. Today, this attractive establishment has a white-painted, creeper-clad exterior and a series of entrance porches which give the impression of it having once been two or three cottages.

Blackbird Inn

With many years experience in the trade, hosts Gill and Ted Anthony have created a warm inviting atmosphere which is enhanced by a blazing log fire in winter. The Blackbird is renowned throughout the area for its fine ales and cuisine. Ted is proud of his record as a cellar-man and serves a pint which is as good as any in the district, and the chef presents a varied and imaginative menu, complemented by a choice of daily specials. A long-standing tradition at the Blackbird has been the Sunday roast, an idea which was popular here long before others thought of it. The inn has two friendly dining rooms, a lively bar and a function room with an optional skittles alley. Supervised children are very welcome, and there is a safe and attractive garden to the rear. *Blackbird Inn, Westbuckland, Near Wellington, Somerset Tel: 01823 461273*

Wellington
Map 5 ref F10
6 miles SW of Taunton on the B3187
The old market town of Wellington lies beside the A38, six miles southwest of Taunton. Once an important producer of woven cloth and serge, the prosperity of the town owed much to Quaker entrepreneurs, and later, the Fox banking family. (Fox, Fowler and Co were the last private bank in England to issue notes, continuing to do so until 1921 when they were taken over by Lloyds.) The broad streets around the centre are peppered with fine Georgian buildings, including the neoclassical town hall, and at the eastern end of the town there is a much-altered Perpendicular-style church which contains the ostentatious tomb of Sir John Popham, the judge who presided at the trial of Guy Fawkes. Another spectacular monument, that to the Duke of Wellington, can be seen on a spur of the Blackdown Hills, three miles to the south; more is written about this in the chapter on South Somerset. Present-day Wellington is a pleasant and prosperous shopping and light industrial centre which enjoys easy access to and from the M5.

Thorne St Margaret
Map 5 ref E10
8 miles SW of Taunton off the A38
The Vale of Taunton Deane, the broad valley between the southern Quantocks and the Devon border, contains some of the most fertile farmland in the county. Thanks to its prolonged agricultural prosperity, the area is dotted with fine country houses. Three that are worthy of note can be found to the west of Wellington in the lanes around the village of Thorne St Margaret. **Cothay**, described by Pevsner as "*one of the most perfect smaller English manor houses of the late 15th century*", stands beside the River Tone a mile to the west of the village; the slightly older **Greenham Barton**, which retains

its early 15th-century two-storey porch and open hall, is situated a mile to the south; and **Wellisford Manor**, which was built of brick around 1700 in a style reflecting the contemporary architecture of nearby Devon, lies half a mile to the north.

Milverton
Map 5 ref F9

6 miles W of Taunton on the B3187

The B3187 to the north of Wellington leads to the sizable village of Milverton, another former weaving centre which has been left with a legacy of elegant Georgian houses. The largely 14th-century red sandstone church of St Michael contains some striking internal features, including a Norman font with characteristic cross and cable carving, a set of choir stalls carved with the twelve apostles, a handsome rood screen, and some fine carved bench ends.

Hill Common
Map 5 ref F9

3 miles W of Taunton on the B3227

The impressive **Baron of Beef Carvery** is situated in the hamlet of Hill Common, on the B3227 midway between Milverton and Taunton. Easily recognised by its white-painted exterior, bright red awning and colourful floral tubs, inside it is a very pleasant eating place which offers a splendid carvery and a la carte menu. The main courses are varied, generous and imaginatively prepared, and many are accompanied by an interesting selection of sauces; also worth noting is the varied selection of vegetarian dishes.

Proprietor Judy Vaessen is a very hands-on host who makes a

Baron of Beef Carvery

feature of offering reduced prices for children of various ages, with two year-olds and under eating free. On the day we called, she was busy preparing for the day's pre-booked reservations, and she also caters for weddings and special occasions. Open Tuesdays to Saturdays 12 noon to 2pm and 7pm to 9.30pm, and Sunday lunchtimes only from 12 noon to 2.30pm. Advance booking advised. *Baron of Beef Carvery, Hill Common, Near Taunton, Somerset   Tel: 01823 400279*

Wiveliscombe
Map 5 ref E9

10 miles NW of Taunton on the B3227

Another large village, Wiveliscombe, lies on the B3227 three miles to the northwest of Milverton. An ancient settlement with a strangely remote atmosphere, the Romans once occupied a fort here and indeed, they left behind a quantity of 3rd and 4th-century coins to prove it. In medieval times, the local manor house was a summer residence of the bishops of Bath and Wells. Its remains, which include a striking 14th-century archway, have now been incorporated into a group of cottages near the church. The red sandstone church was totally rebuilt in the 19th century in a curious neo-Gothic style which is part-Perpendicular, part-18th-century preaching house. During the Second World War, the crypt was used to store priceless historic documents and ecclesiastical treasures which were brought here from parts of the country which were more at risk from aerial attack.

Tolland
Map 5 ref F9

10 miles NW of Taunton off the B3224

Gaulden Manor, Tolland

The B3188 to the north of Wiveliscombe passes to the west of Tolland, the location of the lovely **Gaulden Manor**. The estate dates from the 12th century, although the present house is largely 17th century. It once belonged to the Turberville family, a name borrowed by Thomas Hardy for use in his novel, Tess Of The D'Urbervilles.

Still in use as a family home, the house contains an exceptional collection of period furniture and fine china. The great hall has a superb plaster ceiling and fireplace, and the room known as the chapel boasts a particularly fine oak screen.

Set in a beautiful wooded combe, Gaulden Manor is surrounded by a series of small ornamental enclosures known as the *"Little Gardens of Gaulden"*. These include a scent garden, butterfly garden, rose garden, bog garden and Old Monk's fish pond. (Open Sundays, Thursdays and Bank Holiday Mondays, 2pm to 5.30pm between early-May and early-September; also Easter Sunday and Monday.)

Brendon Hills to the Coast

Monksilver *Map 5 ref E8*

6 miles SE of Minehead off the A358

Another handsome manor house lies the southern edge of Monksilver, three miles to the north on the B3188 Watchet road. Built in the middle of Elizabeth I's reign on the site of a monastic settlement, **Combe Sydenham Hall** was the home of Elizabeth Sydenham, second wife of Sir Francis Drake. According to local legend, after Elizabeth had consented to the marriage, she grew so weary of waiting for Sir Francis to return from his voyages around the world that she resolved to wed another. While on her way to the church, however, a meteorite flew out of the sky and smashed into the ground in front of her, a sign, she thought, that she ought to wait on. The original meteorite, now known as *"Drake's Cannonball"*, is on display in the great hall and is said to bring luck to those who touch it. The 500-acre grounds have been designated a country park and contain a working corn mill complete with water wheel, an Elizabethan-style garden, woodland walks, children's play area and deer park. (Open Sundays to Fridays, 10am to 5pm between early-March and end-October.)

The estate also incorporates a modern trout farm which stands on the site of a fully restored Tudor trout hatchery dating from the end of the 16th century. Here, visitors can purchase fresh rainbow trout, smoked trout and a number of other specialist food products made here under the *"Monksmill"* label. **Nettlecombe Court**, one mile to the west, is an ancient manor which once belonged to the Raleigh family, ancestors of Sir Walter. Later, it passed by marriage to the Cornish Trevelyans, and it is now a field studies centre which is open to visitors on Thursdays only by appointment.

Stogumber
Map 5 ref F8

6 miles SE of Minehead off the A358

The lanes to the east of Monksilver lead through the curiously-named village of Stogumber to Stogumber Halt, one of ten stations on the West Somerset Railway.

Crowcombe
Map 5 ref F8

8 miles SE of Minehead off the A358

One of the loveliest villages in the area, Crowcombe, is situated in the western foothills of the Quantocks, to the east of Stogumber station and the A358 Taunton to Williton road. Once an important stopping place on the road to the Bristol Channel coast, the village has an impressive mainly Perpendicular parish church with a fan-vaulted south porch, a fine south aisle, and a wonderful collection of bench ends, one of which is dated 1534, depicting such curious pagan-looking figures as the green man, a mermaid, and a pair of naked men attempting to spear a dragon. A striking 17th-century family pew of the Carews can be seen in the north transept, and there is also an 18th-century screen, pulpit and altar designed by Thomas Parker.

Parker was also the architect of **Crowcombe Court**, the somewhat down-at-heel looking brick mansion which dominates the village. However, he wasn't able to see his commission through to completion for he was dismissed for stealing coins discovered in the foundations of the previous house which had been declared treasure trove. The village also contains a rare part-Tudor church house which served as a parish hall, and a Jacobean brewery with mullioned windows whose lower floor was later converted to almshouses and whose upper floor became a school.

Williton
Map 5 ref E7

6 miles E of Minehead on the A39

To the northwest of Crowcombe, the A358 runs along the foot of the Quantock ridge to its junction with the A39 at Williton, a former Saxon royal estate which is now a sizable village on the busy holiday route to Minehead and the west Somerset coast. The manor was the home of Sir Reginald Fitzurse, one of Thomas Becket's murderers, who was forced to sell part of it to pay for his journey of repentance to Rome and the Holy Land. The Knights Hospitaller founded an institution here which continued to be known as **Williton Hospital** until the 17th century.

Present-day Williton contains the diesel locomotive workshops of the **West Somerset Railway**, and just off the A39 at **Orchard Mill**, there is a restored water wheel and museum of early farm and domestic equipment which is open Tuesdays to Sundays, 10am to 6pm between early-March and mid-December. A delightful small country manor house, **Orchard Wyndham**, is situated a mile to the southwest of the village. Built in the 14th century and much-altered since, it has been used as a family home by the Wyndhams for the past four and a half centuries. (Guided tours available by appointment during August; telephone 01984 32309.)

Washford   *Map 5 ref E7*
4 miles SE of Minehead on the A39

At Washford, two miles west of Williton, a lane to the south of the A39 leads to the remains of **Cleeve Abbey**, the only monastery in Somerset to have belonged to the austere Cistercian order. The abbey was founded in 1198 by the Earl of Lincoln in the beautiful valley of the River Washford, or "*Vallis Florida*". Many of the great monastic houses were allowed to fall into disrepair following Henry VIII's Dissolution of the Monasteries in 1539. However, the cloister buildings at Cleeve were soon put to domestic use and are now among the most complete in the country.

Despite the cruciform abbey church having been reduced to its foundations, the refectory, chapter house, monks' common room, dormitory and cloisters remain remarkably intact. Most impressive of all is the great hall, a magnificent building with tall windows and a wagon roof which is decorated with busts of crowned angels, moulded wall plates, medieval murals, and a unique set of floor tiles with heraldic designs. The curved dormitory staircase with its archways and mullioned windows is particularly fine, and the combined gatehouse and almonry, the last building to be constructed before the Dissolution, makes an imposing entrance to the abbey precinct. (Open daily, 10am to 6pm between 1 April and 31 October; Wednesdays to Sundays, 10am to 4pm between 1 November and 31 March.)

Treborough   *Map 4 ref E8*
6 miles S of Minehead off A39

To the south of Cleeve Abbey and towards Treborough, the land rises into the **Brendon Hills**, the upland area within the Exmoor National

Park lying to the east and north of the River Exe. During the mid 19th century, iron ore was mined in significant quantities above the village of Treborough, then carried down a steep mineral railway to the coast for shipment to the furnaces of South Wales. At one time almost 1000 people were employed by the Ebbw Vale Company, strict Nonconformists who imposed a rigorous teetotal regime on their workers. (Those wanting a drink had to walk across the moor all the way to Raleigh's Cross.)

The company also founded a miners' settlement with a temperance hotel and three chapels, which became renowned for the achievements of its choir and fife and drum band. Sections of the old mineral railway can still be made out today, such as the one near the junction of the A39 and the B3190 to the east of Washford, and the two-mile stretch leading down to the coast at Watchet is now a pleasant footpath. The Brendon Hills also offer some fine walking through attractive woodland and open moorland, and further south, the surprisingly well-assimilated **Wimbleball and Clatworthy Reservoirs** offer some good facilities for picnickers, anglers and watersports enthusiasts.

Watchet   *Map 5 ref E7*
4 miles E of Minehead on the Coast

Watchet, a small town on the coast to the north of Washford, has been a port since Saxon times. In the 6th century, St Decuman is reputed to have landed here from Wales, bringing with him a cow to provide sustenance, and in the 9th and 10th centuries, the settlement was important enough to have been sacked by the Vikings on at least three occasions. By the 17th century, Watchet had become an important paper manufacturing centre, and by the mid 19th, around 30,000 tons of iron ore from the Brendon hills were being exported each year through its docks. Coleridge's imaginary crew set sail from here in *"The Rime Of The Ancient Mariner"*, the epic poem which was written when the author was residing at nearby Nether Stowey.

Unlike many similar-sized ports which fell into disuse following the arrival of the railways, Watchet docks has somehow managed to survive. Despite the total decline in the iron ore trade, sizable cargo vessels continue to tie up here to be loaded with goods bound for the Iberian peninsula and elsewhere.

The scale of Watchet's parish church reflects the town's long-standing importance. Set well away from the centre, it contains several fine tombs to members of the Wyndham family, the local lords of the manor who did much to develop the economic potential of the locality. One 16th-century family member, Florence Wyndham, had to be buried twice: the day after her first funeral, the church sexton went down to the vaults to surreptitiously remove a ring from her finger and the old woman suddenly woke up. In recent years, Watchet has also developed as something of a coastal resort whose attractions include an interesting small museum dedicated to local maritime history.

Blue Anchor Bay
Map 4 ref E7
3 miles E of Minehead on the Coast

A more developed seaside resort can be found three miles to the west at Blue Anchor Bay, a broad arc of sand named after a 17th-century inn, not the colour of the water. The bay is well known for its fossils, both palaeontological and living, and boasts a fine sandy beach which, sadly, is marred by caravan sites and seaside attractions of the gaudier variety.

Carhampton
Map 4 ref E7
3 miles SE of Minehead on the A39

The atmosphere is very different at Carhampton, one mile to the southwest, a small inland village on the A39 which was the site of a Viking victory in the 9th century. The original church was named after St Carantoc, an early Celtic missionary from across the Bristol Channel who is reputed to have chosen the site for his ministry by throwing his wooden altar overboard and following it to the shore. The present structure, though much restored, contains a remarkable 15th-century painted screen which extends across the entire church. The old inn near the churchyard lych gate has the date 1638 set into its cobbled floor in sheep's knuckle bones.

Each January, the residents of Carhampton re-enact the ancient custom of *"wassailing the apple trees"*. A toast is made to the most productive tree in the district and cider is poured onto its trunk in a charming ceremony which is probably pagan in origin. A local folk tale tells of mysterious Madame Carne, a Carhampton woman who died in 1612 after having done away with three husbands. According to the legend, her ghost returned home after her funeral to prepare breakfast for the mourners.

Dunster
Map 4 ref D7
2 miles S of Minehead on the A396

The ancient fortified settlement of Dunster has an almost fairy-tale appearance when approached along the A39 from the southeast. With its huge turreted castle rising above the trees and distinctive ruined folly on nearby Conygar hill, it is a place well-worth visiting, particularly out of season. ***Dunster Castle*** was founded by William de Mohun on a natural promontory above the River Avill a few years before the Domesday Book was compiled in 1086. In 1404, it passed to the Luttrells for the then colossal sum of 5000 marks, about £3300, in whose family it remained until Lt. Col. G W F Luttrell presented the property to the National Trust in 1975.

Dunster Yarn Market and Castle, Dunster

During the English Civil War, Dunster Castle was one of the last Royalist strongholds in the West Country to fall, the garrison finally surrendering after a siege lasting 160 days. The castle underwent some major alterations during the latter part of the 17th century and some of its finest internal features date from this period, including the superb plasterwork ceiling in the dining room, and the magnificent balustraded main staircase with its delicately-carved flora and fauna. The banqueting hall contains a unique collection of 16th-century leather hangings, and there are also many fine examples of period furniture throughout the interior.

Further changes to the building by Anthony Salvin in the 19th century completed the transformation from castle to country mansion. Work on the steeply-terraced garden with its striking collection of rare shrubs and subtropical plants was also carried out at this time. Dunster Castle is surrounded by an attractive 28-acre park containing an 18th-century flour mill which was built on the site of a Norman predecessor. Restored to working order in 1979, **Dunster Working Water Mill** continues to produce flour and other cereals for wholesale and retail sale. Dunster Castle is open Saturdays to Wednesdays, 11am to 5pm between late-March and end-October; grounds open daily, all year round. The water mill is open Sundays to Fridays, 10.30am to 5pm between 1 April and 31 October (also Saturdays in July and August.)

The old feudal settlement of Dunster has a wide main street which is dominated by the castle. At the northern end stands the former **Yarn Market**, a small octagonal building erected by the Luttrells around 1600 when the village was a centre of the cloth trade. Indeed, such was its importance that at one time, Dunster gave its name to a type of woollen cloth which was renowned for its quality and strength. The nearby **Luttrell Arms** is over a century older; a private residence which was converted to an inn around 1650, it has a fine 15th-century porch and a room lined with carved oak panelling. It once belonged to Cleeve Abbey, as did the 14th-century nunnery in Church Street. Dunster's principal medieval monastic house, **Dunster Priory**, was an outpost of Bath Abbey. Now largely demolished, the only parts to survive are its splendid priory church and unusual 12th-century dovecote. This can be seen in a nearby garden and still contains the revolving ladder which was used to reach the roosting birds. (Open daily between Easter and mid-October.)

Dunster's former priory church is now one of the finest parish churches in Somerset. Rebuilt of rose pink sandstone by the monks after 1100, its 100ft tower was added in the 15th century at a cost of *13s 4d per foot, with an extra 20s for the pinnacles.* The building's most outstanding internal feature is its fan vaulted rood screen which extends across the nave and aisles, one of the widest and most impressive of its kind in the country. There are also some fine 15th and 16th-century fittings, an unusual painting of the Brazen Serpent thought to be by Thornhill, and several monuments to members of the Luttrell family. On the southern edge of the village, the River

Avill is spanned by the ancient **Gallox Bridge**, a medieval packhorse bridge which is now under the care of English Heritage.

Minehead

Map 4 ref D7

10 miles NE of Taunton on the A39

Two miles to the northwest of Dunster, the West Somerset Railway terminates at Minehead, a popular seaside town lying at the foot of the wooded promontory known as North Hill. Despite sounding like a product of the industrial age, this is one of the oldest settlements in the county, having been a busy Bristol Channel port since the time of the Celts. The old harbour lies in the lee of North Hill, making it one of the safest landing places in the West Country. At one time, ships would arrive here with their cargoes of wool and livestock from Ireland, crops from the plantations of Virginia, coal from the valleys of South Wales, and day trippers from Cardiff and Bristol. Today, however, the merchantmen and paddle steamers have gone and the harbour is the peaceful haunt of sailing dinghies and pleasure craft.

The Old Ship Aground

Situated on Minehead seafront and enjoying a magnificent harbour view is the **Old Ship Aground**, an attractive public house which is thought to be the only one in the country to bear this unusual name.

The present building started out in 1894 as the Pier Hotel, and it wasn't until 1977 that its name was changed to that of an old inn which once stood on the quay. Today, this impressive pub and eating place is run by Tony and Sue, friendly hosts who offer a warm welcome to locals and visitors from all over the world. All are provided with genuine hospitality, fine traditional ales and an extensive menu of delicious home-cooked meals which are served in the atmosphere of a traditional English pub. For those wishing to stay in this delightful area of northwest Somerset, the Old Ship Aground also has seven comfortable en suite guest rooms available. *The Old Ship Aground, Quay Street, Minehead, Somerset Tel: 01643 702087*

A good view of the old port can be had from the **North Hill Nature Trail**, a three-mile walk which starts near the lifeboat station on the harbourside. Minehead's parish church of St Michael stands in a prominent position below North Hill. A substantial part 14th-century building, in past centuries a light was kept burning in the tower to help guide ships into the harbour. The interior contains a number of unusual features, including a rare medieval prayer book, or missal, which once belonged to the Richard Fitzjames, a local vicar who went on to become Bishop of London in 1506.

Minehead's 19th-century decline as a port was offset by its gradual expansion as a seaside resort. The local powers that be went to great pains to attract a suitably respectable clientele, and indeed a local bylaw was in force until 1890 which forbad anyone over ten years of age from swimming in the sea *"except from a bathing machine, tent, or other effective screen."* The arrival of the railway in 1874 failed to trigger the brutal expansion experienced by some other seaside resorts, and during the First World War, Minehead was able to provide an escape from the ravages of war at timeless establishments like the Strand Hotel, where guests were entertained by such stars as Anna Pavlova and Gladys Cooper.

Improvements to Minehead have been gradual. In the 1920s, an impressive municipal park known as **Blenheim Gardens** was built near the seafront which incorporates *"Little England"*, a model country town with its own miniature railway and floodlights. The most momentous change, however, came in 1962 when Billy Butlin opened a holiday camp at the eastern end of the esplanade. Now updated and renamed **Somerwest World**, this popular attraction has done much to transform present-day Minehead into an all-round family resort.

Minehead to the Exmoor National Park

Selworthy *Map 4 ref D7*

3 miles W of Minehead off the A39

For those wishing to avoid Minehead's summer crush, a particularly fine walk sets out westwards over North Hill and continues on to **Selworthy Beacon**, part of the 12400-acre Holnicote Estate. The estate covers four and a half miles of coastline between Minehead and Porlock Bay and is now owned by the National Trust. At Hurlstone Point, the South West Coast Path curves inland to avoid the possibility of landslips in the soft Foreland Sandstone before dropping down to Bossington; however, there is an alternative, more arduous clifftop path which should be attempted by experienced walkers only.

Selworthy

The Holnicote Estate extends over five miles inland to the 1700ft Dunkery Beacon, the highest point on Exmoor. It also incorporates fifteen farms, many of them on the high moor, and a number of small settlements, including Selworthy, a superb model village of whitewashed cob and thatch cottages which was built by Sir Thomas Dyke-Acland to house his estate workers. The churchyard on the hill offers a fine view of Dunkery Beacon, and there is also a National Trust information centre here which is open daily, 10am (2pm Sundays) to 5pm between late-March and end-October.

Allerford
Map 4 ref C7
5 miles W of Minehead on the A39
Allerford, one mile to the west, is a lovely old village which has some fine stone cottages and an elegant twin-arched **Packhorse Bridge**. Located in Allerford's old school, the **West Somerset Museum** is an imaginatively presented museum of rural life whose exhibits include a Victorian kitchen, laundry and dairy, and an old schoolroom complete with desks, books and children's toys. (Open Mondays to Saturdays, 10.30am to 4.30pm between 1 April and 31 October.) From Allerford, it is possible to climb back up the hill for the return walk to Minehead, a round trip of about twelve miles. Alternatively, both villages can be reached by car from the A39. For those preferring a walk on the high moor, a spectacular circular nature walk starts and finishes at the Webber's Post car park at the foot of Dunkery Hill.

Porlock
Map 4 ref C7
6 miles W of Minehead off the A39
To the west of Allerford, the A39 winds through the narrow streets of Porlock, an ancient settlement once frequented by Saxon kings which in recent decades has become a popular riding and holiday centre. The village is filled with lovely old buildings, most notably the 15th-century **Doverhay Manor** with its striking traceried hall window, and the largely 13th-century red sandstone parish church with its curious truncated shingle spire, the top section of which was lost in a 17th-century thunderstorm. The church also contains an exceptional font, an unusual Easter sepulchre, and a remarkable double tomb consisting of almost life-size alabaster effigies of Sir John Harrington, who was knighted by Henry V during the Agincourt campaign, and his wife, who lived on for over half a century after Sir John's death in 1418.

Porlock has long had the feel of a community at the end of the world thanks to its position at the foot of **Porlock Hill**, the notorious incline which carries the A39 onto Exmoor. The road rises 1350ft in under three miles and in places has a gradient of 1 in 4. A less challenging toll road winds its way through the Lovelace estate from **Porlock Weir**, a hamlet lying on the coast a mile and a half to the northwest of Porlock. Now a small tide-affected harbour populated by pleasure craft, this was once an important seaport. The Danes sacked it on a number of occasions in the 10th century, and in 1052, Harold, the future king of England, landed here from Ireland to begin a career which ended at the Battle of Hastings. Now peaceful and picturesque, Porlock Weir offers a number of interesting attractions, including a working blacksmith's forge, a picture gallery, and a glass studio which provides visitors with the opportunity to see lead crystal being made in the traditional manner. A submerged forest, a relic of the last Ice Age, lies a short distance offshore and can be glimpsed at low tide.

Culbone   *Map 4 ref B6*
8 miles W of Minehead on the A39

From Porlock Weir, a pleasant mile-long walk leads up through the woods to **Culbone Church**, the smallest church in England still in regular use. A true hidden gem which measures only 33ft by 14ft, this superb part-Norman building is set in a delightful wooded combe which once supported a small charcoal-burning community. Inside, there is a fine 14th-century screen and some handsome carved benches.

From Culbone church, the coastal footpath continues on to the Devon border at County Gate, one of several spectacular viewpoints on this dramatic stretch of coastline. Here, the great whale's back hills of Exmoor plunge into the sea, giving breathtaking views across the Bristol Channel to South Wales. One of the few Roman remains on Exmoor, a lookout station for observing cross-Channel raiding parties, lies on a headland to the north of the car park.

Doone Valley   *Map 4 ref B7*
10 miles W of Minehead off the A39

To the south of County Gate lies the scenic **Doone Valley**, a long enclosed sweep of green pasture and mature woodland which was immortalised by R D Blackmore in his classic romantic novel, Lorna Doone. The now-demolished medieval farm known as Hoccombe Combe is thought to have been the home of a wild and unruly Exmoor family whose real-life exploits provided the inspiration for the story. The beautiful little 15th-century church at Oare is thought to be the setting of the heroine's dramatic interrupted wedding. Inside, there is a fine set of 19th-century box pews and an unusual piscina shaped like a man's head.

Exmoor National Park   *Map 4 ref B7/8*
SW of Minehead

The characteristic heartland of the Exmoor National Park, seventy per cent of which lies within Somerset, is a high treeless plateau of hard-wearing Devonian shale which has been carved into a series of steep-sided valleys by the prolonged action of the moor's many fast-flowing streams. Whereas the upland vegetation is mostly heather, gorse and bracken, the more sheltered valleys are carpeted with grassy meadows and pockets of woodland. The deep wooded combes also provide shelter for herds of shy red deer which roam at will, but are seldom seen. Easier to spot are the hardy Exmoor ponies, now almost all cross-breeds, which often congregate at roadside parking areas where there can be rich pickings from holidaymakers.

Exmoor is criss-crossed by a network of paths and bridleways which provide some superb opportunities for walking and pony-trekking. Many follow the routes of the ancient ridgeways across the high moor and pass close to the numerous hut circles, standing stones, barrows and other Bronze and Iron Age remains which litter the landscape. Among the finest examples are the stone circle on Porlock Hill, **Alderman's Barrow** north of Exford, and the delightfully-named **Cow Castle** near Simonsbath. The remarkable medieval packhorse bridge known as **Tarr Steps** lies to the north of the village of Hawkridge, near Dulverton. A superb example of a West Country clapper bridge, it is composed of massive flat stones placed across solidly-built dry stone uprights. The Roman relic known as the **Caractacus Stone** can be seen a couple of miles to the east of here near Spire Cross.

Tourist Information Centres

Centres in bold are open all the year around.

Bath
Abbey Chambers, Abbey Church Yard, Bath , Avon, BA1 1LY
Tel: 01225 462831

Bridgwater
50 High Street, , Bridgwater, Somerset, TA6 3BL
Tel: 01278 427652

Bristol Airport
Bristol Airport, Avon, BS19 3DY
Tel: 01275 474444

Bristol
St Nicholas Church, St Nicholas Street, Bristol, Avon, BS1 1UE
Tel: 0117 9260767

Burnham on Sea
South Esplanade, Burnham on Sea, Somerset, TA8 1BU
Tel:01278 787852

Chard
The Guildhall, Fore Street, Chard, Somerset, TA20 1PP
Tel: 01460 67463

Cheddar
The George, Cheddar, Somerset, BS27 3QE
Tel: 01934 744071

Frome
The Round Tower, Justice Lane, Frome, Somerset, BA11 1BB
Tel: 01373 467271

Glastonbury
The Tribunal, 9 High Street, Glastonbury, Somerset, BA6 9DP
Tel: 01458 832954

Gordano
Junction 19 / M5, Gordano, Gordano, Avon, BS20 9AX
Tel: 01275 975516

Minehead
17 Friday Street, , Minehead, Somerset, TA24 5UB
Tel: 01643 702624

Podimore
Somerset Visitor Centre, Forte Services (A303), Podimore
Somerset, BA22 8JG
Tel: 01935 841302

Sedgemoor Services
Somerset Visitor Centre, Sedgemoor Services M 25 (South),
Sedgemoor Services, Somerset, BS26 2UF
Tel: 01934 750833

Taunton
Paul Street, , Taunton, Somerset, TA1 3PF
Tel: 01823 336344

Wells
Town Hall, Market Place, Wells, Somerset, BA5 2RB
Tel: 01749 672552

Weston super Mare
Visitor Information Centre, Beach Lawns, Weston super Mare
Avon, BS23 1AT Tel: 01934 626838

Yeovil
Petter's House, Petter's Way, Yeovil, Somerset, BA20 1SH
Tel: 01935 71279

Index

The Hidden Places Series

ORDER FORM

To order more copies of this title or any of the others in this series
please complete the order form below and send to:

**Travel Publishing Ltd,.7a Apollo House, Calleva Park
Aldermaston, Berks, RG7 8TN**

Title	P9rice	Quantity	Value
Channel Islands	£6.99	....	....
Devon & Cornwall	£4.95	....	....
Dorset, Hants & Isle of Wight	£4.95	....	....
East Anglia	£4.95	....	....
Gloucestershire	£6.99	....	....
Heart of England	£4.95	....	....
Lancashire & Cheshire	£4.95	....	....
Lake District & Cumbria	£4.95	....	....
North Wales	£4.95	....	....
Northumberland & Durham	£4.95	....	....
Peak District	£6.99	....	....
Potteries	£6.99	....	....
Somerset	£6.99	....	....
South East	£4.95	....	....
South Wales	£4.95	....	....
Thames & Chilterns	£5.99	....	....
Welsh Borders	£5.99	....	....
Wiltshire	£6.99	....	....
Yorkshire & Humberside	£4.95	....	....
England	£9.99	....	....
Ireland	£8.99	....	....
Scotland	£8.99	....	....
Wales	£8.99	....	....
	TOTAL	_____	_____

**For orders of less than 10 copies please add £1 per book for
postage & packing. Orders over 10 copies P & P free.**

I enclose a cheque for £ .... made payable to Travel
Publishing Ltd

NAME ....

ADDRESS ....

....

POSTCODE ....

TEL NO ....

The Hidden Places Series
READER REACTION FORM

The Hidden Places research team would like to receive reader's comments on any visitor attractions or places reviewed in the book and also recommendations for suitable entries to be included in the next edition. This will help ensure that the **Hidden Places** series continues to provide its readers with useful information on the more interesting, unusual or unique features of each attraction or place ensuring that their stay in the local area is an enjoyable and stimulating experience.

To provide your comments or recommendations would you please complete the forms below as indicated and send to: **The Research Department, Travel Publishing Ltd., 7a Apollo House, Calleva Park, Aldermaston, Reading, RG7 8TN.**

Please tick as appropriate: Comments ☐ Recommendation ☐

Name of *"Hidden Place"*:

Address:

Telephone Number:

Name of Contact:

Comments/Reason for recommendation:

Name of Reader:

Address:

Telephone Number:

The Hidden Places Series
READER REACTION FORM

The Hidden Places research team would like to receive reader's comments on any visitor attractions or places reviewed in the book and also recommendations for suitable entries to be included in the next edition. This will help ensure that the ***Hidden Places*** series continues to provide its readers with useful information on the more interesting, unusual or unique features of each attraction or place ensuring that their stay in the local area is an enjoyable and stimulating experience.

To provide your comments or recommendations would you please complete the forms below as indicated and send to: **The Research Department, Travel Publishing Ltd., 7a Apollo House, Calleva Park, Aldermaston, Reading, RG7 8TN.**

Please tick as appropriate: Comments ☐ Recommendation ☐

Name of *"Hidden Place"*:

Address:

Telephone Number:

Name of Contact:

Comments/Reason for recommendation:

Name of Reader:

Address:

Telephone Number:

MAP SECTION

These maps are small scale extracts from the Wessex Official Tourist Map, reproduced with permission of Estates Publications

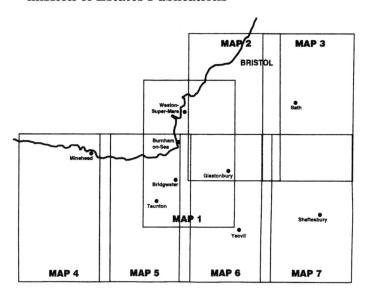

The following pages of maps encompass the main cities, towns and geographical features of the area of Somerset, which is covered by this guide.

Every place, whether it be a city, town or village, featured in the book is incorporated in the maps.

Distances are indicated by the use of scale bars on each of the maps

MAP 1

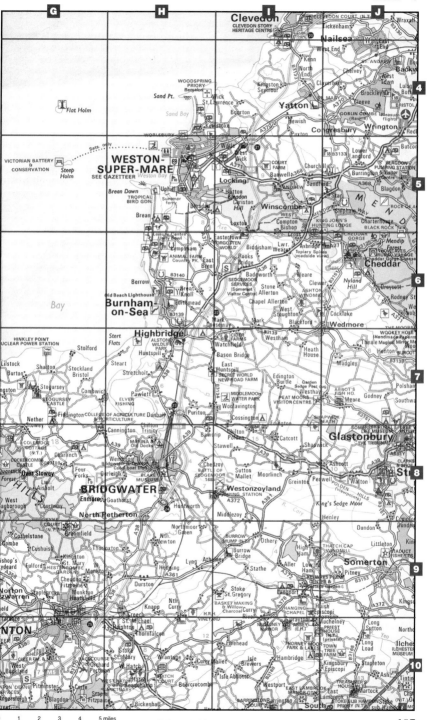

MAP 2

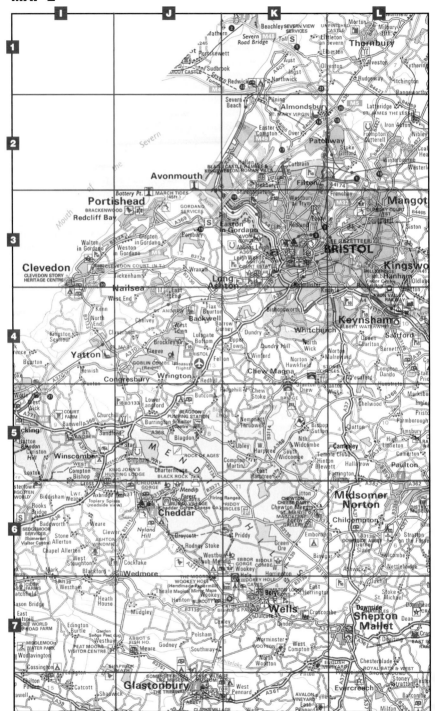

MAP 3

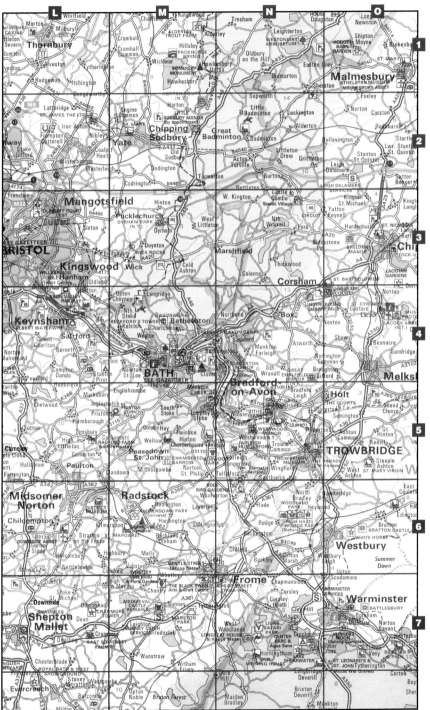

MAP 4

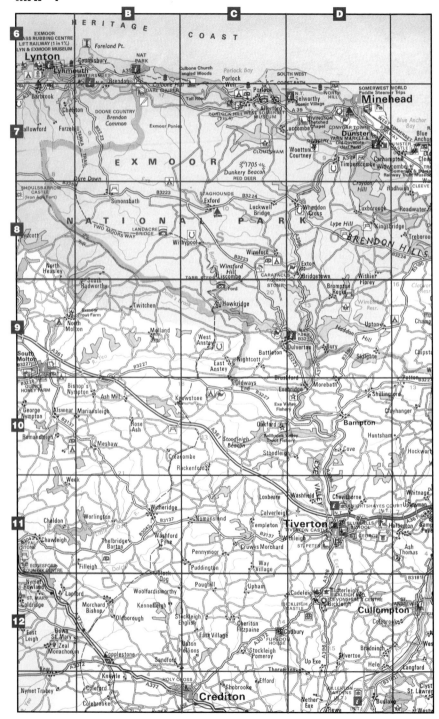

©Estate Publications   Crown Copyright Reserved

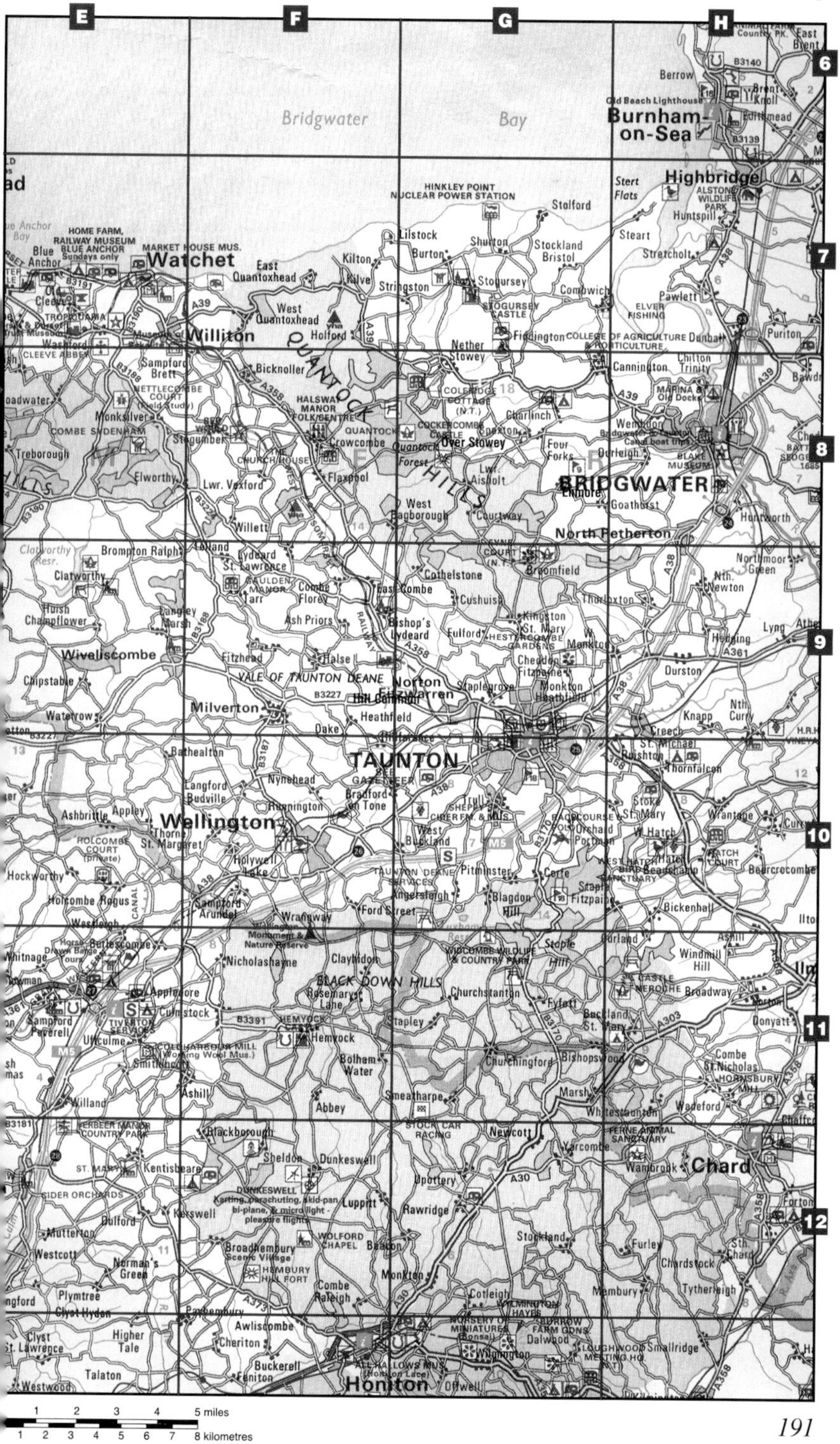

MAP 5

E   F   G   H

6

Bridgwater   Bay

Berrow

Old Beach Lighthouse
**Burnham-
on-Sea**

East
Brent

B3140

Brent
Knoll

Rooksbridge

7

Blue Anchor
Bay
Blue Anchor
HOME FARM,
RAILWAY MUSEUM
BLUE ANCHOR
Sundays only
MARKET HOUSE MUS.
Watchet
MUSEUM
Old
Cleeve
TROPIQUARIA
Bardon Mill Museum
WASHFORD
CLEEVE ABBEY

East
Quantoxhead
West
Quantoxhead
Williton

Lilstock
Kilton
Alve
Burton
Holford

Shurton
Stringston
Stogursey
STOGURSEY
CASTLE

HINKLEY POINT
NUCLEAR POWER STATION

Stolford
Stockland
Bristol
Combwich
Fiddington

Stert
Flats
Steart
Stretcholt

COLLEGE OF AGRICULTURE
& HORTICULTURE

Huntspill

Highbridge

ALSTONE
WILDLIFE
PARK

ELVER
FISHING
Dunball
Pawlett
Puriton

Chilton
Trinity

MARINA
Old Docks
Down End

Bawdrip

8

Sampford
Brett
NETTLECOMBE
COURT (Tudor)
Monksilver
Treborough
Elworthy
EXMOOR
COMBE SYDENHAM

Bicknoller
HALSWAY
MANOR
FOLK CENTRE
Stogumber
CHURCH HOUSE
Crowcombe

QUANTOCK HILLS

Flaxpool

COLE
COTTAGE
(N.T.)
QUANTOCK
Forest
Over Stowey
West
Bagborough
Aisholt

Nether
Stowey

Charlinch

Four
Forks
Enmore
Courtway
Goathurst

Cannington

Wembdon
Durleigh
Catch boat trip

BRIDGWATER

BLAKE
MUSEUM

Hamworth

North Petherton

9

Clatworthy
Resr.
Clatworthy
Hurst
Champflower

Brompton Ralph
Tolland
Lydeard
St. Lawrence
COMBE
FLOREY

Langley
Marsh
Wiveliscombe
Chipstable
Waterrow
B3227

Ash Priors
Fitzhead
Halse
Milverton

VALE OF TAUNTON DEANE
B3227
Dske

Cothelstone
East
Combe
Cushuish
Bishop's
Lydeard

Fulford

Combe
KINGSTON
ST. MARY
HESTERCOMBE
GARDENS

Heathfield

Cheddon
Fitzpaine
Monkton
Heathfield

Broomfield

Thurloxton

Cheddon
Fitzpaine
Monkton

Nth.
Newton
Hedging
Durston

Northmoor
Green

Lyng

A361
Athe

9

Bathealton
Nynehead
Bradford
on Tone

TAUNTON

St. Michael
Ruishton
Thornfalcon

Knapp

Nth.
Curry
Creech
H.R.N.

Ashbrittle
Appley
Langford
Wellington
St. Margaret
Runnington
GALMINGTON
Bradford
on Tone

West
Buckland
CHERRY & HILLS
TAUNTON DEANE
SERVICES

RACECOURSE
Pitminster
Orchard
Portman

Stoke
St. Mary
Hatch

Wrantage

10

Hockworthy
HOLCOMBE
COURT
(Tudor)
Holcombe
Rogus
Wasleigh

Holywell
Lake
Sampford
Arundel

Angersleigh
Wrangway
Ford Street

Corfe
Blagdon
Pitminster

West
Hatch
Beercombe
Bickenhall

HATCH
COURT
Beercrocombe
Ilto

Whitnage
Howman
Butterleigh
Burlescombe
Appledore
Culmstock

BLACK DOWN HILLS

Nicholashayne
Claybidon
Rosemary
Lane

CASTLE
NEROCHE

Windmill
Hill

Broadway

Ilm

11

Sampford
Peverell
TIVERTON
Uffculme
CULM VALLEY
(Working Wool Mus.)
Smithincott
Willand

HEMYOCK
Hemyock
Stapley

Bolham
Water

Churchstanton

Fyfett
Buckland
St. Mary

Churchinford
Bishopswood

A303

Donyatt
St. Nicholas
HORNSBURY
MILL

12

Ashill
mas

Blackborough
Sheldon

Kentisbeare
CIDER ORCHARDS
St. Mary's
Kentisbeare
Mutterton
Westcott
Norman's
Green
Plymtree
Clyst Hydon
B3181
PEMBER MANOR
COUNTRY PARK

Dunkeswell
STOCK CAR
RACING

Newcott
Yarcombe

FERNE ANIMAL
SANCTUARY
Wambrook
Chard
Forton
St.
Chard

Smeatharpe
Abbey
DUNKESWELL
Karting, parachuting, skid-pan,
bi-plane & microlight
pleasure flights

Luppitt
Rawridge

Stockland

Marsh
Wadeford
Whitestaunton

Chardstock
Tytherleigh

Chaffc

Dulford
WOLFORD
CHAPEL
Beaton
Broadhembury
SCENIC VILLAGE
HEMBURY
HILL FORT

Monkton

Upottery

Cotleigh

Membury

Luton
Higher
Tale
Talaton

Payhembury
Awliscombe
Cheriton
Feniton
Buckerell
Offwell
Wilmington
Honiton
Combe
Raleigh
ALL HALLOWS MUS.
(Honiton Lace)
WROUGHTON
MINIATURE
RAILWAY
Bonsai
Dalwood
FARROW
FARM GDNS
COMBE
HOUSE
Smallridge
CLOUGHWOOD
MEETING HO.

Clyst
St. Lawrence
Westwood

1 2 3 4 5 miles
1 2 3 4 5 6 7 8 kilometres

MAP 6

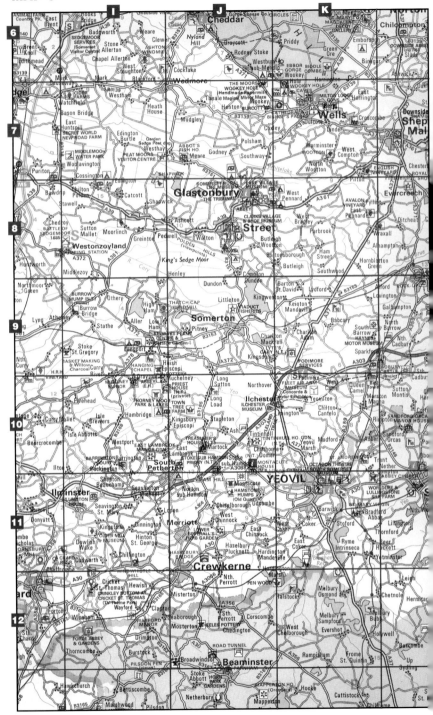

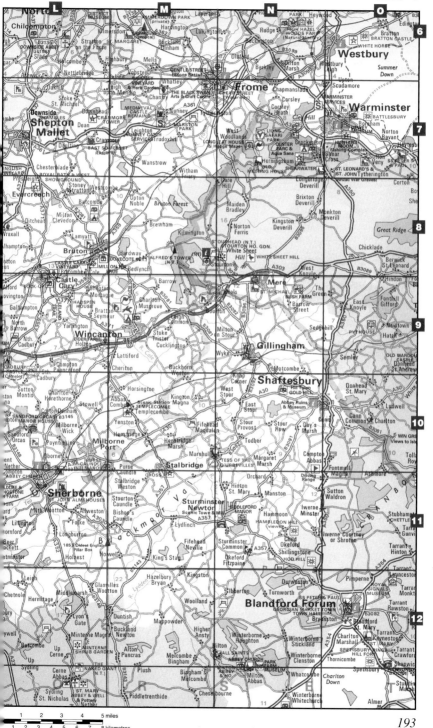

MAP 7